Carlile P. Patterson

An Attempt to Solve the Problem of the First Landing Place

of Columbus in the New World

Carlile P. Patterson

An Attempt to Solve the Problem of the First Landing Place of Columbus in the New World

ISBN/EAN: 9783744711807

Printed in Europe, USA, Canada, Australia, Japan

Cover: Foto ©ninafisch / pixelio.de

More available books at **www.hansebooks.com**

UNITED STATES
COAST AND GEODETIC SURVEY

CARLILE P. PATTERSON
SUPERINTENDENT

METHODS AND RESULTS

AN ATTEMPT TO SOLVE THE PROBLEM

OF THE

FIRST LANDING PLACE OF COLUMBUS

IN THE NEW WORLD

APPENDIX No. 18—REPORT FOR 1880

WASHINGTON
GOVERNMENT PRINTING OFFICE
1882

AN ATTEMPT TO SOLVE THE PROBLEM OF THE FIRST LANDING PLACE OF COLUMBUS IN THE NEW WORLD.

By Capt. G. V. FOX, Assistant Secretary of the Navy from May, 1861, to November, 1866, Member of the Massachusetts Historical Society, etc.

I.

INTRODUCTION.

The discovery of America by Christopher Columbus is, perhaps, the most important event recorded in secular history. Ancient philosophers had suggested the sphericity of the earth, the zone of water, and the theoretical possibility of reaching the Indies by sailing west; and Columbus recalled these suggestions before the great councils that ridiculed and rejected his proposal.

The art of navigation is as old as civilization, and the practice of it must have begun when bartering commenced. Its early development in European waters was, probably, in the eastern part of the Mediterranean, with open boats, such as Homer mentions. Vessels of this character could not make a commercial nation like that which throve in Phœnicia. Therefore we find that her ships were large and that they used both sails and oars.[1] More than three thousand years ago the sailors of this little state had passed out of the Mediterranean, had founded Cadiz, and were trafficking along the Atlantic shores of Europe and Africa.

The maritime spirit of the Phœnicians descended upon the Carthagenians, the Italians, and the Portuguese. The last named began that golden age of geographical discovery which characterized the fifteenth century.

All navigators antecedent to Columbus followed the same way in searching for new countries. They crept along the shores of contiguous lands making no discoveries beyond unless by chance, through the stress of storms, or by the letting loose of birds.

The Vikings tribe of Norway were an exception. The area of sheltered fiords in their fretted coast exceeds all the arable land in the country. Hardy venturesome seamen grew here from the law of environment, and their vessels also were evolved in a tempestuous ocean and by means of a business very different from trade. In shape these resembled the present whale-boats,[2] which are proved to be the best type for rough seas.

A well-preserved specimen, supposed to have been made about the tenth century, was dug out of a tumulus at Gogstad, Norway, in the spring of 1880.[3] It is 72 feet long, 17 wide, and it probably drew 5 feet of water. There are twenty benches for rowers. Near the middle is a wooden step for a mast, and indications that this might have been lowered at will. The vessels of the Northmen were obviously good sea-boats and from their light draft and the alternative of oars, they must have been very handy in the neighborhood of land, but under canvas they could make no headway unless by " sailing large."

The Phœnicians used the Pole Star in navigating and the ancient mariners of Ceylon regulated their track through the ocean by observing the flight of the birds which they set free at intervals.[4] In this mode, and also from being forced to scud in gales, the Northmen extended

---

[1] Ezekiel xxvii, 5–7 [about 588 B. C.]. Probably this time was the height of her power.
[2] See frontispiece. *Denmark in the Early Iron Age.* London, 1866. C. Engelhardt.
[3] See *La Nature* for 1880.
[4] *History of Merchant Shipping and Ancient Commerce.* W. S. Lindsay; 4 vols. London, 1874. Vol. I, pp. 14 and 359.

their discoveries until finally, in a storm, they saw Greenland in the ninth century and Labrador in the tenth. There is a sequence of land across, which points out the successive steps they took. West 180 miles from Norway, are the Shetlands; thence west-northwest 170, to the Faroes; 240 miles farther, on the same course, lies Iceland; and northwesterly, 165 more, is Greenland. The longest distance is from this to Labrador, 500 miles, whence the coast-line is continuous.

It is indisputable that the Northmen were the ablest seamen and boldest navigators of ancient times; but they were neither traders nor colonizers. The lands which they discovered in the west were supposed to be an extension of the European Continent. They derived no advantage from them, neither did the world. In the graceful language of Washington Irving, "If the Norsemen saw the New World, it was but a transient glimpse, leading to no certain or permanent knowledge, and in a little time lost again to mankind.([1])

Columbus was an efficient seaman and also a religious enthusiast—a rare combination. In his correspondence with Toscanelli, in 1474, is the first mention of his decision to seek the Indies by sailing west. Three years afterward he visited the northern regions, Iceland probably, where he must have found the tradition of western discoveries, although the secret of the Sagas was not published until the last half of the sixteenth century. Whatever he learned there had no influence upon his previous resolution. He did not propose to hunt after the lands which the Northmen had discarded. His purpose was to open a way, by water, to the rich and populous countries spoken of by Marco Polo, for this was linked in his mind with the propagation of the Christian faith and the rescue of the Holy Sepulchre from the Infidels.

Everything essential to such a voyage had been ready for a long time through the growth of navigation. In the previous century, Edward III, of England, had good, stout, sailing ships and plenty of seamen. The mariner's compass was in use as early as 1100–1250 A. D.([2]) Latitude by observation was familiar to sailors (see Appendix D) and "dead reckoning" of some kind had always been practiced. Parallels and meridians were applied in the second century. Columbus himself made maps, and globes are mentioned in his journal. His plan, and the reasoning by which he supported it, seem clear enough now; but then every council rejected it. In his letter to the King and Queen of Spain, narrating his fourth voyage, the Admiral wrote: "For seven years was I at your royal court, where every one to whom the enterprise was mentioned treated it as ridiculous; but now there is not a man, down to the very tailors, who does not beg to be allowed to become a discoverer."([3])

His first proposal was to the King of Portugal, to steer west from Lisbon. This would have taken him to America, at a point five miles south of Cape Henlopen; distance, 3,095 miles. Japan is 9,801 miles west from Lisbon; but along the great circle, which goes through Europe and Siberia, it is only 5,768 miles.

Columbus gives no reason for going to the Canary Islands to take his final departure. Irving says it was the damaged state of the Pinta's rudder that led him to go there to exchange it;([4]) but on the day he sailed from Spain, August 3, 1492, he entered in his journal that he was steering for the Canaries,([5]) and the mishap to the Pinta was not till the 6th of August.([6]) Martin Behem's globe and Toscanelli's map agreed in placing Cipango (Japan) due west from the Canaries. Columbus knew these facts, and his desire to steer across the ocean *in the same latitude*, was accordant to a usage of navigators which has been given up only since the introduction of chronometers. His going to the Canary Islands was providential, because a west course from there is within the influence of the trade winds, of which he was ignorant, and these wafted him continuously onward, while his crew were grumbling at his persistence. If he had sailed west from Lisbon, or from Palos, he would have been antagonized by variable, and by westerly winds, thus lengthening the passage and thereby adding to the discontents of the men, all of which might have compelled him to abandon his voyage.

([1]) *Irving's Columbus.* Revised edition, 1854. Vol. I, Introduction, p. 2.
([2]) *Hallam's Middle Ages.* Vol. III, p. 394; and *Ersch und Grüber's Encycl.* III, p. 392.
([3]) *Coleccion de los Viages y Descubrimientos, etc. Navarrete.* Madrid, 1825. Tomo I, p. 311.
([4]) *Irving's Columbus.* Revised edition, 1854. Vol. I, p. 130.
([5]) See Appendix D.
([6]) See *Navarrete.* Tomo I, p. 4, August 6; also *prologue*, pp. 2–3.

In his first log across the Atlantic, he likened the weather to that of Andalusia in April. It lacked nothing, he said, except the songs of the nightingales. Such it has been, where he crossed, for æons of time. On this route the vessels of the Crusaders might have gone to America in the twelfth century with less peril than they went from England to Joppa then.

In recent years small boats from the United States have arrived safe in England, in spite of bad weather and faulty observations.

The unfolding of physical laws has dissipated the artificial terrors of the ocean; but in the time of Columbus superstition and ignorance brooded there, making it truly a "sea of darkness," which the imagination only had pierced.

The world is not indebted to the wisdom of the learned for the eventful voyage that opened the oceans to commerce, and continents to trade and settlement. To Columbus belongs the merit of this inestimable boon. He inspired the wise and good Queen Isabella[1] equally with the humble sailors of Palos to put their trust in his scheme. He was as persistent in maintaining it through the rebuffs of eighteen years as he was steadfast in holding to his predetermined course across the Atlantic.

It takes not a jot from the glory of his discovery that he underestimated the size of the earth; or that he died in ignorance of the transcendent importance of his deed; or that the Northmen had preceded him. The fulfilment of his design, to steer west until he reached the Indies or found intervening land, was the triumph of human reasoning; it was the soul's work, into which neither chance nor the fickle winds intruded.

The aim of this monograph is to try to solve the problem of the first landing-place of Columbus in the New World. It is founded, as all others are, upon Las Casas's (abridged) copy of the "log-book", or journal, of Columbus. Nothing has been raked from the arcana of the past to impeach this; and it will continue to be used until the original journal is produced or this copy is shown to be spurious.

It is manifest that no landfall, or track, can stand which is supported by assertions that are in opposition to Las Casas's narrative. Knowing this to be true I have tested in the following pages every track, by placing paragraphs from each author and from the journal in juxtaposition so that any one, with the help of the correct appendix chart, shall discern the contradictions.

The selection of a new landfall and track through the Bahamas, different from all hitherto ascribed to Columbus, is the natural result of this sifting. The track which I have laid down was chosen because it appears to be the only one that can be made to fit the courses, distances, and descriptions in the log-book.

WASHINGTON, D. C., *May* 31, 1881.

---

[1] Columbus wrote—*Navarrete*, Vol. I, p. 266—"In the midst of the general incredulity the Almighty infused into the Queen, my lady, the spirit of intelligence and energy, and while every one else, in his ignorance, was expatiating only on the inconvenience and cost, her Highness approved of it, on the contrary, and gave it all the support in her power."

NARRATIVE AND DISCUSSION.

Columbus made four voyages to the New World. The first was from the village of Palos, which he left on Friday, the 3d day of August, 1492, with a squadron of three small vessels and about ninety men. The largest vessel was the Santa Maria, his flag-ship; the next, the Pinta, commanded by Martin Alonso Pinzon; and the smallest, the Niña, under command of Vincente Yañez Pinzon, a brother of Martin. He went directly to the Canaries, where he arrived August 12, and he refitted and reprovisioned his vessels there. Thursday, the 6th of September, he sailed from the harbor of St. Sebastian, in the island of Gomera, but was becalmed among the Canaries until Saturday night, when he met the usual northeast wind and steered west, his predetermined course for the Indies. He crossed the Atlantic and made the land at 2 a. m., Friday, the 12th of October (old style).[1] After sunrise he landed and took formal possession of a small island of the Lucayos [Bahamas], called by the natives Guanahani, but named by him San Salvador. The 15th and 16th of October he visited and named the second island Santa Maria de la Concepcion. The 17th and 18th, and part of the 19th, he was at the third, named by him Fernandina. Part of the 19th, and to the 24th, he explored the shores of the fourth, which he thought the natives called Saometo, but he gave it the name of Isabella. On the 26th he anchored south of seven or eight islands which he called, Sand Islands. Leaving these early on the 27th he brought his squadron to anchor Sunday, the 28th of October, in a harbor of Cuba; this island he named Juana. From this date until December 5 he examined the northeast coast, and the harbors of Cuba; then he crossed over to Hayti, which he called Española. While exploring the harbors and north shore the Santa Maria was wrecked on the evening of December 24, near the present Layeul Bay. This calamity led Columbus to make a settlement from the crew in this bay.

He left here on the 4th of January, 1493, and followed the coast to the bay of Samana. Hence, on the 16th of January, he sailed for Spain. On the 18th he arrived at the Azores, and left there the 24th. On the 4th of March he was compelled by stress of weather to put into Lisbon. He sailed thence the 13th, and on Friday the 15th of March, after an absence of two hundred and twenty-four days, he returned in the Niña, to Palos.

He sailed on his second voyage from Cadiz, Wednesday, the 25th of September, 1493, with three large vessels and fourteen small ones, and about 1,500 men. He anchored at the Canaries and remained from the 1st to the 13th of October; thence, steering more to the southward than on his first voyage, on Sunday the 3d of November he discovered an island which he named Dominica. From here he steered to the northward and westward, visited several of the Caribbean Islands, Porto Rico, north side of Hayti, south side of Cuba, Jamaica, the south side of Hayti, around the east end to the north side, thence to the island of Guadaloupe, and on the 10th of March he left there for Spain and anchored at Cadiz June 11, 1496.

On his third voyage he sailed from San Lucar May 30, 1498, with six vessels; he touched at Porto Santo, Madeira, the Canaries, and anchored June 27 at the Cape de Verd Islands. He left there July 5 and steered still more to the southward, which brought him on the 31st of July to an island which he named Trinidad. The next day, while coasting the south shore, he discovered the continent of South America. He continued along the main land until August 14, when he stood over to Hayti where he was detained for more than a year by the disorganized condition of affairs.

On the 23d of August, 1500, a new governor-general, Don Francisco de Bobadilla, arrived. His instructions were so vague that his wicked heart construed them to permit him to put irons upon the limbs of the discoverer of the New World, and in this pitiable condition Columbus arrived at Cadiz on the 25th of November, 1500.

His fourth and last voyage was also from Cadiz. Leaving there on the 8th of May, 1502, with four small vessels and 150 men he touched on the coast of Morocco, sailed from the Canaries May 25, and anchored at Martinique[2] June 15; thence along Santa Cruz and Porto Rico, and on the 29th

---

[1] If the Gregorian Calendar of 1582, but which is reckoned from the Council of Nice, is applied to Columbus's discovery, it will make the date Friday, the 21st day of October.

[2] Irving and Major say Martinique; Nararrete says Santa Lucia.

of June he arrived on the south side of Hayti; left there July 14, touched at the Morant Cays, and the islands south of Cuba which he had visited on his second voyage, and then to the small island of Guanaja, or Bonacca, from which on the 30th of July, 1502, he saw, for the first time, the continent of North America. He then followed the coast of Central America and the coast of the Isthmus of Panama to the Gulf of Darien until the 1st of May, 1503, when he sailed for Hayti, but owing to the strong westerly current he brought up among the small islands on the south of Cuba where he had anchored the year before. Near the end of June he put into Jamaica, and his vessels being unseaworthy he remained there until June 28, 1504, when he was rescued and taken to Hayti. On the 12th of September he sailed for Spain and arrived at San Lucar November 7, 1504. He died at Valladolid on the 20th of May, 1506.

From this brief summary of the voyages of Columbus to the New World we learn that he visited and named five islands of the Lucayos on his first voyage, but that he remained among them only fifteen days; all his other voyaging was along the coasts and to the islands which border the Caribbean Sea. He never returned to the Lucayos, nor are they often mentioned in the contemporaneous narrations. Within a few years after the death of Columbus, King Ferdinand authorized the transportation of laborers from them to Hayti, to work the mines there. In this way the whole population perished. In the Bahamas, at the present time, there are no descendants of the simple natives described by Columbus.

The chart which he made of the Lucayos, the declarations in writing which signified his formal possession of Guanahani, the journal which he kept for "Their Highnesses," and all the original documents essential to authenticate this historical point, have disappeared.

The contemporaries and acquaintances of Columbus, Peter Martyr, Andres Bernaldes, G. F. de Oviedo, Marco A. Sabelico, Augustus Giustiniani, and his son Fernando, whose writings, or copies thereof, are preserved, give no information which will assist the student to determine the island upon which he first landed. There are four that have been pointed out and argued for most earnestly, which I shall enumerate. Beginning at the southeast the first is Grand Turk Island, in latitude 21° 31' north, longitude 71° 08' west from Greenwich. It is 5½ by 1¼ miles, has 6.87 square miles, is generally low, with an elevation at the highest part of 70 feet; bare of trees, and about one-third of the surface is salt and fresh water lagoons. This place is affirmed by Don M. F. de Navarrete, *Coleccion de los Viages y descubrimientos que hicieron por mar los Españoles desdes fines del siglo*, XV, Madrid, 1825, Tomo I, and supported by Samuel Kettell, *Personal Narrative of the First Voyage of Columbus to America*, Boston, 1827. George Gibbs, *Proceedings of the New York Historical Society*, 1846, Appendix; and R. H. Major, *Select Letters of Columbus*, edition of 1847, London.

The second island is that of Mariguana. The east end is latitude 22° 17' north, longitude 72° 39' west from Greenwich. It is 23½ miles long and from 2 to 6½ wide; has about 96 square miles, and is low, with the exception of a hill near the middle 101 feet high, and another at the east end 90 feet. There are neither lakes nor lagoons on the island. This is put forward by Fr. Adolph de Varnhagen, who published in Chili, in 1864, a work called *La Verdadera Guanahani de Colon*. He republished it in 1869 at Vienna.

The third is Watling's Island. The latitude of the southeast point is 23° 55' north, longitude 74° 28' west from Greenwich. Length north and south 13 miles, and breadth about 5 to 7. It has 60 square miles. Near the center is a hill of 140 feet. A lagoon of brackish water takes up one third of the island. Juan Bautista Muñoz first chose Watling in his *Historia del Nuevo Mundo*, Madrid, 1793, Tomo I. He is sustained by Capt. A. B. Becher, Royal Navy, author of *Land Fall of Columbus*, London, 1856. O. Peschel, *Geschichte des Zeitalters der Entdeckungen*, Stuttgart and Augsburg, 1858; and R. H. Major, *Journal of the Royal Geographical Society*, vol. XLI, May 8, 1871, wherein he recants his former approval of Grand Turk and adopts that of Captain Becher.

The fourth island is that known as Cat, or San Salvador. The southeast end is latitude 24° 09' north, longitude 75° 18' west from Greenwich. Northwest and southeast it is 43 miles, and the breadth 2½ to 3½ miles. At the southeast end a part runs west-southwest 10 miles, with a width of 3½. There are 100 square miles in it. At the northwest end the hills rise to 400 feet, and are the highest land in the Bahamas. It has neither lakes nor lagoons. The principal writers who have adopted Cat are Catesby, *Natural History of Carolina*, 1731. *A New Collection of Voyages and*

Travels, J. Knox, London, 1767. An elaborate note in the *Second Volume of the French Translation of Navarrete, p.* 339, Paris, 1828; the author of this note is Mr. De La Roquette. *Revue nautique du premier voyage de Christophe Colomb au nouveau monde par* M. le Baron de Montlezun, *Nouvelles Annales des Voyages et des Sciences Géographiques, Deuxième Série,* Tome X, Paris, 1828, and Tome XII, Paris, 1829. Washington Irving, *Life and Voyages of Christopher Columbus,* London, 1828, revised edition, New York, 1848; in the third volume of this edition, appendix, p. 380, Irving gives the authorship of his track to the late Commander Alexander Slidell Mackenzie, United States Navy. Baron Alexander von Humboldt argues, most ably, in favor of the route selected by Irving and Mackenzie, in *Examen critique de l'histoire de la géographie du nouveau continent,* 1837.

Irving and Humboldt, as well as some other writers, allege that Cat Island has the sanctity of tradition in favor of it. An impression to this effect certainly prevails, but as those who have adopted it do not give their authority, I can only offer to the reader that which freed my mind from its influence. The Spaniards were the discoverers of the New World; they made the first maps of the West Indies; for a long time they were the exclusive explorers there; they obtained, and have now, more of the lore of these regions than can be found among all other nations. If any tradition truly exists it ought to be found in Spain, in the writings of her historians. None of those I have cited mention it. On the contrary, Muñoz and Navarrete, who had access to the documents of Columbus and his contemporaries, and who each pointed out a landfall, differ; neither selecting Cat (*ante,* p. 7), which is proof that there is no tradition in relation to it to in the country which alone could give it legitimate birth.

It is true that some maps can be referred to in support of a claim for Cat. But the identification of Guanahani, or San Salvador, with Cat is not earlier than the seventeenth century. Perhaps the first is on *Atlas Minor, by Blaeu, West Indies,* 1635, which is the same as a map published by *Joannes de Laet,* at *Leyden,* 1625, titled, *Nieuwe Wereldt.* They are identical also in *Blaeu's Atlas,* Tome XII, *Continent de l'Amérique,* Amsterdam, 1667. In the eighteenth century more maps were published, and the identity of Cat with San Salvador received additional support. See *Map of North America by* John Senex, Charles Price, and John Maxwell, 1710; *North America and West Indies,* by Emanuel Bowen, 1733?; D'Anville, *Map of* 1746; *The West India Atlas,* by the late Thomas Jefferys, 1775; Laurie and Whittle, 1794; and a Spanish *Chart of the Antilles,* by Langara, 1799.)

In Major's ~~landfall~~ (pp. 207–210) are collated the ancient and modern names of most of the Bahamas, ten of which he asserts can be identified. I cite only such as I wish to use in my argument:

He says that Guanahani is the present Watling; Guanima the present Cat or San Salvador; Mayaguana the present Mariguana; and Samana, the present Samana or Atwood Cay.

He considers that the identification of these four, as well as the other six, involves the whole question of the landfall, and he is so certain of it that he puts Senhor de Varnhagen "out of court" (p. 208), because his Marignana appears on the old maps *with* Guanahani.

Major does not furnish ~~the~~ evidence to enable us to see that Guanahani is Watling. He refers to Herrera's map of 1601, with the expectation that we shall be as easily satisfied as he was. Looking at this map I notice three little islands marked "triangula," and northwest of them is Guanahani.

Map of New Spain, Nicolas Vallard, 1547, and on plate x and plate lxii of the *Munich Collection,* 1592, this Triango appears.

Map of America and West Indies, Anthony Jacobsz, 1621, we find Triangulo.

Dutch Chart, Hesselgerritz, about 1650, and map of 1650, Sanson d'Abbeville, there is Triangulo.

In Ottens's *Atlas Minor,* vol. iv, titled *Nova Tabula exhibens insulas, etc.,* there is a map which is the same as a map published by d'Anville in *Charlevoix's Histoire de l'isle Espagnole,* Paris, 1730. On these maps we find Triangolo *on Watlins I.*

On Robt. Sayer's *Map,* November 1, 1792, and in *Jeffery's Atlas,* 1794, there is *El triangulo, Watlands or Watling.*

These citations prove that the old maps, and especially Herrera's, to which Major calls attention, had two islands placed near each other which were called, respectively, Guanahani and triango, or Triangulo. It is the former that Major says is the present Watling; but from these maps it appears that *triango*, or *Triangulo*, is that now called Watling.

The earliest date I have found for Guanima [Cat] is a map in the Jomard collection styled *Mappe Monde Peinte sur parchmen par ordre Henri II. Roi de France (I. l'artie)*. M. D. Avezae makes the date of this 1532. Here are Guanima, Mayuana [Mariguana], and one little island intermediate, to which are applied the *two names* of "Guanahani", "Samana." This is remarkable, as showing a connection between them at an early date.

A great part of the maps of the sixteenth and seventeenth centuries have Guanima and Maya-guana as outside islands, with Guanahani lying between; and inside of these is placed Samana. Triangulo or triango appears, but not so often. All this indicates that the information transmitted to the early map-makers included the fact that Guanahani or San Salvador was an island *distinct* from Guanima [Cat], Mayaguana [Mariguana], Triangulo [Watling], and Samana. This last is asserted to be the present Samana or Atwood Cay but I hope to prove, ~~later~~, that it was the ancient name of the Crooked Island group, and thus save myself from being, as Major said of Varn-hagen, " put out of court."

The valuable map of La Cosa, which I shall remark upon, fixed the position of Guanahani about the middle of the northeast side of the Bahamas. Herrera and others copy it. Such a situa-tion is so mathematically conspicuous, and so easily followed, that we ought to find Guanahani or San Salvador retained here on ~~later~~ maps, in spite of the alterations involved in improved cartog-raphy. This has been the case. In the absence of determining data as to which one was the true San Salvador, this name has been applied, fortuitously, to several neighboring islands, but with the exception of Navarrete's chart, the *location* is where the companion of Columbus put it.

The old charts can be appealed to in corroboration of parts of this investigation, but consenta-neity in respect to the first landfall will never be reached by their evidence. Fortunately a copy of Columbus's journal in the Bahamas has been preserved, but it has been construed so differently that all the authors of the four tracks referred to found their arguments upon this document.

About 1790, Navarrete, a civil officer of the marine department of Spain, found in the archives of the Duke del Infantado a manuscript narrative of the first voyage of Columbus, abridged from the original. It proved to be in the handwriting of Bishop Las Casas, a contemporary and com-panion of Columbus, who had visited the new world several times. He wrote a general history of the Indies, in three volumes, from the discovery in 1492 to 1520, which ~~exists only in manuscript, but it has been, and is, accessible to scholars.~~ Las Casas was engaged upon this history from 1527 to 1559; and he had before him the original journals of Columbus, his map of the first discovery, and many letters and documents, now lost. In the year 1825 the Spanish Government published this precious narrative, together with other valuable papers relating to Columbus. It is a matter of sincere regret that Las Casas abridged, in any degree, the "log-book" of such an eventful voyage, but we are thankful that he transcribed Columbus's words literally, from the landfall at Guanahani to the 29th of October, because it is only this part that is essential to prove the true landing-place.

Kettell has translated into English all of Las Casas's abridgement of Columbus's first voyage, and Irving, Major, and Captain Becher such parts as they considered necessary to their respective arguments. Here will be found the Spanish text from the first edition of Navarrete, 1825, vol. I, pp. 18–42, in parallel columns with the English by Mr. H. L. Thomas, translator of the United States State Department, at Washington. With respect to the disputed parts of the journal care has been taken to have a strict rendering of the Spanish.

App. 18——2

Miercoles 10 de Octubre.

Navegó al Ouesudueste, anduvieron á diez millas por hora y á ratos doce y algun rato á siete, y entre dia y noche cincuenta y nueve leguas: contó á la gente cuarenta y cuatro leguas no mas. Aquí la gente ya no lo podia sufrir: quejábase del largo viage; pero el Almirante los esforzó lo mejor que pudo dándoles buena esperanza de los provechos que podrian haber. Y añadia que por demas era quejarse, pues que él habia venido á las Indias, y que así lo habia de proseguir hasta hallarlas con el ayuda de nuestro Señor.

Jueves 11 de Octubre.

Navegó al Ouesudueste, tuvieron mucha mar mas que en todo el viage habian tenido. Vieron pardelas y un junco verde junto á la nao. Vieron los de la carabela Pinta una caña y un palo, y tomaron otro palillo labrado á lo que parecia con hierro, y un pedazo de caña y otra yerba que nace en tierra, y una tablilla. Los de la carabela Niña tambien vieron otras señales de tierra y un palillo cargado descaramojos([1]). Con estas señales respiraron y alegráronse todos. Anduvieron en este dia hasta puesto el sol veinte y siete leguas.

Despues del sol puesto navegó á su primer camino al Oeste: andarian doce millas cada hora, y hasta dos horas despues de media noche andarian noventa millas, que son veinte y dos leguas y media. Y porque la carabela Pinta era mas velera é iba delante del Almirante, halló tierra y hizo las señas quel Almirante habia mandado. Esta tierra vido primero un marinero que se decia Rodrigo de Triana; puesto que el Almirante á las diez de la noche, estando en el castillo de popa, vido lumbre, aunque fue cosa tan cerrada que no quiso afirmar que fuese tierra; pero llamó á Pero Gutierrez, repostero destrados del Rey, ó díjole, que parecia lumbre, que mirase el, y así lo hizo y vídola: díjolo tambien á Rodrigo Sanchez de Segovia quél Rey y la Reina enviaban en el armada por veedor, el cual no vido nada porque no estaba en lugar dó la pudiese ver. Despues quel Almirante lo dijo se vido una vez ó dos, y era como una candelilla de cera que se alzaba y levantaba, lo cual á pocos pareciera ser indicio de tierra. Pero el Almirante tuvo por cierto estar junto á la tierra. Por lo cual cuando dijeron la Salve, que la acostumbran decir ó

([1]) Por de escaramujos.

He sailed west-southwest, at the rate of ten miles an hour and occasionally twelve, and at other times seven, running between day and night fifty nine leagues: he told the men only forty four. Here the crew could stand it no longer, they complained of the long voyage, but the Admiral encouraged them as best he could giving them hopes of the profits that they might have. And he added that it was useless to murmur because he had come to [in quest of?] the Indies, and was so going to continue until he found them with God's help.

Thursday October 11th.

He sailed to the west-southwest, had a high sea, higher than hitherto. They saw pardelas([1]) and floating by the vessel a green rush. The men of the Pinta saw a reed and a stick, and got a small stick apparently cut or worked with an iron instrument, and a piece of cane and some other grass which grows on the land, and a small board. Those of the Caravel Niña also saw other indications of land and a little stick loaded with dog roses. In view of such signs they breathed more freely and grew cheerful. They ran until sunset of that day twenty seven leagues. After sunset he sailed on his first course to the West: they went about twelve miles an hour, and two hours after midnight they had run about ninety miles, that is twenty two and a half leagues. As the Caravel Pinta was a better sailer and had the lead, she made land and showed the signals ordered by the Admiral. The land was first seen by a sailor called Rodrigo de Triana:([2]) as the Admiral at ten o'clock at night standing on the castle of the poop saw a light, but so indistinct that he did not dare to affirm that it was land; yet he called the attention of Pero Gutierrez, a King's butler to it, and told him that it seemed to be a light, and told him to look, he did so and saw it: he did the same with Rodrigo Sanchez de Segovia, whom the King and Queen had sent with the fleet as supervisor and purveyor, but

([1]) Pardelo—a name given by the Spanish to a bird of a gray color, or white and black. *Dominguez Dictionary*—Madrid 1878.

([2]) It was first discovered by a mariner named Rodriguez Bermejo, resident of Triana, a suburb of Seville, but native of Alcala de la Guadaira; but the reward was afterwards adjudged to the Admiral, for having previously perceived the light. *W. Irving's Abridged Columbus*. New York, 1847. p. 60.

cantar á su manera todos los marineros y se hallan todos, rogó y amonestólos el Almirante que hiciesen buena guarda al castillo de proa, y mirasen bien por la tierra, y que al que le dijese primero que via tierra le daria luego un jubon de seda, sin las otras mercedes que los Reyes habian prometido, que eran diez mil maravedis de juro á quien primero la viese. A las dos horas despues de media noche pareció la tierra, de la cual estarian dos leguas. Amañaron(¹) todas las velas, y quedaron con el treo(²) que es la vela grande sin bonetas, y pusiéronse á la corda(³) temporizando hasta el dia Viernes que llegaron á una isleta de los Lucayos, que se llamaba en lengua de indios *Guanahani*(⁴). Luego vieron gente desnuda, y el Almirante salió á tierra en la barca armada, y Martin Alonso Pinzon y Vicente Anes(⁵), su hermano, que era capitan de la Niña. Sacó el Almirante la bandera Real y los capitanes con dos banderas de la Cruz Verde, que llevaba el Almirante en todos los navíos por seña con una F y una Y: encima de cada letra su corona, una de un cabo de la ✠ y otra de otro. Puestos en tierra vieron árboles muy verdes y aguas muchas y frutas de diversas maneras. El Almirante llamó á los dos capitanes y á los demas que saltaron en tierra, y á Rodrigo Descovedo, Escribano de toda el armada, y á Rodrigo Sanchez de Segovia, y dijo que le diesen por fe y testimonio como él por ante todos tomaba, como de hecho tomó, posesion de la dicha isla por el Rey é por la Reina sus señores, haciendo las protestaciones que se requirian, como mas largo se contiene en los testimonios que allí se hicieron por escripto. Luego se ayuntó allí mucha gente de la isla. Esto que se sigue son palabras forma-

he, not being in a good position for seeing it, saw nothing. After the Admiral said this it was seen once or twice, and it was like a small wax candle that was being hoisted and raised, which would seem to few to be an indication of land. The Admiral however was quite convinced of the proximity of land. In consequence of that when they said the *Salve*, which they used to say and sing it in their way, all the sailors and all being present, the Admiral requested and admonished them to keep a sharp look out at the castle of the bow, and to look well for land, and said that he would give to him who first saw land a silk doublet, besides the other rewards that the King and Queen had promised, namely an annual pension of ten thousand maravedis(¹) to him who should see it first. Two hours after midnight the land appeared, about two leagues off. They lowered all the sails, leaving only a storm square sail, which is the mainsail without bonnets, and lay to until Friday when they reached a small island of the Lucayos, called *Guanahani* by the natives. They soon saw people naked, and the Admiral went on shore in the armed boat, also Martin Alonso Pinzon and Vincente Anes,(²) his brother, who was commander of the Niña. The Admiral took the Royal standard and the captains with two banners of the Green Cross, which the Admiral carried on all the ships as a distinguishing flag having an F and a Y: each letter surmounted by its crown, one at one arm of the cross, and the other at the other arm. As soon as they had landed they saw trees of a brilliant green abundance of water and fruits of various kinds. The Admiral called the two captains and the rest who had come on shore, and Rodrigo Descovedo, the Notary of all the fleet, and Rodrigo Sanchez de Segovia, and he called them as witnesses to certify that he in presence of them all, was taking, as he in fact took possession of said island for the King and Queen his masters, making the declarations that were required as they will be found more fully in the attestations then taken down in writing. Soon after a large crowd of natives congregated there. What follows are the Admiral's own words in his book on the first voyage and discovery of these Indies. "In order to win the friendship and affection of that people, and be.

(¹) *Amañaron* por *amainaron.*

(²) *Treo*, vela cuadrada que se ponia solo cuando habia mal tiempo para correr.

(³) *Ponerse á la corda*, es ponerse al pairo ó atravesando para no andar ni decaer del punto en que se está.

(⁴) Examinado detenidamente este diario, sus derrotas, recaladas, señales de las tierras, islas, costas y puertos, parece que esta primera isla que Colon descubrió y pisó, poniéndole por nombre *S. Salvador*, debe ser la que está situada mas al Norte de las turcas llamada *del Gran Turco.* Sus circunstancias conforman con la descripcion que Colon hace de ella. Su situacion es por el paralelo de 21°. 30', al Norte de la medianía de la isla de Santo Domingo.

(⁵) Debe decir *Yañes.*

(¹) One cent equals 2.7625 maravedis. *Irving's Columbus*, revised edition 1848. Appendix p. 381.

(²) It ought to be Yañez. Navarreto.

les del Almirante, en su libro de su primera navegacion y descubrimiento de estas Indias. „Yo (dice él) porque nos tuviesen mucha amistad, porque conoscí que era gente que mejor se libraria y convertiria á nuestra Santa Fé con amor que no por fuerza; les dí á algunos de ellos unos bonetes colorados y unas cuentas de vidrio que se ponian al pescuezo, y otras cosas muchas de poco valor con que hobieron mucho placer y quedaron tanto nuestros que era maravilla. Los cuales despues venian á las barcas de los navíos adonde nós estabamos, nadando y nos traían papagoyos y hilo de algodon en ovillos y azagayas, y otras cosas muchas, y nos las trocaban por otras cosas que nós les dabamos, como cuentecillas de vidrio y cascabeles. En fin todo tomaban y daban de aquello que tenian de buena voluntad. Mas me pareció que era gente muy pobre de todo. Ellos andan todos desnudos como su madre los parió, y tambien las mugeres, aunque no vide mas de una farto moza, y todos los que yo ví eran todos mancebos, que ninguno vide de edad de mas de treinta años: muy bien hechos, de muy fermosos cuerpos, y muy buenas caras: los cabellos gruesos cuasi como sedas de cola de caballos, ó cortos: los cabellos traen por encima de las cejas, salvo unos pocos de tras que traen largos, que jamas cortan: dellos se pintan de prieto, y ellos son de la color de los canarios, ni negros ni blancos, y dellos se pintan de blanco, y dellos de colorado, y dellos de lo que fallan, y dellos se pintan las caras, y dellos todo el cuerpo, y dellos solos los ojos, y dellos solo el nariz. Ellos no traen armas ni las cognocen, porque les amostré espadas y las tomaban por el filo, y se cortaban con ignorancia. No tienen algun fierro: sus azagayas son unas varas sin fierro, y algunas de ellas tienen al cabo un diente de pece, y otras de otras cosas. Ellos todos á una mano son de buena estatura de grandeza, y buenos gestos, bien hechos; yo vide algunos que tenian señales de feridas en sus cuerpos, y les hice señas que era aquello, y ellos me amostraron como allí venian gente de otras islas que estaban acerca y les querian tómar, y se defendian; y yo creí, ó creo, que aqui vienen de tierra firme á tomarlos por captivos. Ellos deben ser buenos servidores y de buen ingenio, que veo que muy presto dicen todo lo que les decia, y creo que ligeramente se harian cristianos, que me pareció que ninguna secta tenian. Yo, placiendo á nuestro Señor, levaré de aquí al tiempo de mi partida seis á V. A. para que deprendan fablar.

cause I was convinced that their conversion to our Holy Faith would be better promoted through love than through force; I presented some of them with red caps and some strings of glass beads which they placed around their necks, and with other trifles of insignificant worth that delighted them and by which we have got a wonderful hold on their affections. They afterwards came to the boats of the vessels swimming, bringing us parrots cotton thread in balls and spears, and many other things, which they bartered for others we gave them, as glass beads and little bells. Finally they received every thing and gave whatever they had with good will. But I thought them to be a very poor people. All of them go about naked as when they came into the world, even the women, although I saw but one very young girl, all the rest being young men, none of them being over thirty years of age: their forms being very well proportioned, their bodies graceful and their features handsome: their hair is as coarse as the hair of a horse's tail and cut short: they wear their hair over their eye brows except a little behind which they wear long, and which they never cut: some of them paint themselves black, and they are of the color of the Canary islanders, neither black nor white, and some paint themselves white, and some red, and some with whatever they find, and some paint their faces, and some the whole body, and some their eyes only, and some their noses only. They do not carry arms and have no knowledge of them, for when I showed them the swords they took them by the edge, and through ignorance, cut themselves. They have no iron: their spears consist of staffs without iron, some of them having a fish's tooth at the end, and others other things. As a body they are of good size, good demeanor, and well formed; I saw some with scars on their bodies, and to my signs asking them what these meant, they answered in the same manner, that people from neighboring islands wanted to capture them, and they had defended themselves; and I did believe, and do believe, that they came from the main land to take them prisoners. They must be good servants and very intelligent, because I see that they repeat very quickly what I told them, and it is my conviction that they would easily become Christians, for they seem not to have any sect. If it please our Lord, I will take six of them from here to your Highnesses on my departure, that they may

Ninguna bestia de ninguna manera vide, salvo papagayos en esta isla." Todas son palabras del Almirante.

Sabado 13 de Octubre.

„Luego que amaneció vinieron á la playa muchos destos hombres, todos mancebos, como dicho tengo, y todos de buena estatura, gente muy fermosa: los cabellos no crespos, salvo corredios y gruesos, como sedas de caballo, y todos de la frente y cabeza muy ancha mas que otra generacion que fasta aquí haya visto, y los ojos muy fermosos y no pequeños, y ellos ninguno prieto, salvo de la color de los canarios, ni se debe esperar otra cosa, pues está Lesteoueste con la isla del Hierro(¹) en Canaria so una línea. Las piernas muy derechas, todos á una mano, y no barriga, salvo muy bien hecha. Ellos vinieron á la nao con almadías, que son hechas del pie de un árbol, como un barco luengo, y todo de un pedazo, y labrado muy á maravilla segun la tierra, y grandes en que en algunas venian cuarenta ó cuarenta y cinco hombres, y otras mas pequeñas, fasta haber dellas en que venia un solo hombre. Remaban con una pala como de fornero, y anda á maravilla; y si se le trastorna luego se echan todos á nadar, y la enderezan y vacian con calabazas que traen ellos. Traían ovillos de algodon filado y papagayos, y azagayas, y otras cositas que seria tedio de escrebir, y todo daban por cualquiera cosa que se los diese. Y yo estaba atento y trabajaba de saber si habia oro, y vide que algunos dellos traían un pedazuelo colgado en un agujero que tienen á la nariz, y por señas pude entender que yendo al Sur ó volviendo la isla por el Sur, que estaba allí un Rey que tenia grandes vasos dello, y tenia muy mucho. Trabajó que fuesen allá, y despues vide que no entendian en la ida. Determiné de aguardar fasta mañana en la tarde, y despues partir para el Sudueste, que segun muchos dellos me enseñaron decian que habia tierra al Sur y al Sudueste y al Norueste, y questas del Norueste les venian á combatir muchas veces, y asi ir al Sudueste á buscar el oro y piedras preciosas. Esta isla es bien grande y muy llana y de árboles muy verdes, y muchas aguas, y una laguna en medio muy grande, sin ninguna montaña, y toda ella verde, ques placer de mirarla; y esta gente farto mansa, y por la gana de haber de nuestras cosas, y teniendo que no se les ha de dar sin

(¹) La verdadera situacion de esta isla respecto á la del Hierro es O. 5° S. — E. 5° N.

learn to speak. I have seen here no beasts whatever, but parrots only." All these are the words of the Admiral.

Saturday October 13th.

"At dawn many of these men came down to the shore, all are, as already said, youths of good size and very handsome: their hair is not wooly, but loose and coarse like horse hair, they have broader heads and foreheads than I have ever seen in any other race of men, and the eyes very beautiful not small, none of them are black, but of the complexion of the inhabitants of the Canaries, as it is to be expected, for it is east [and] west with the island of Hierro in the Canaries in the same line. All without exception have very straight limbs, and no bellies, and very well formed. They came to the ship in canoes, made out of trunks of trees all in one piece, and wonderfully built according to the locality, in some of them forty or forty five men came, others were smaller, and in some but a single man came. They paddled with a peel like that of a baker, and make wonderful speed; and if it capsizes all begin to swim and set it right again, and bail out the water with calabashes which they carry. They brought balls of spun cotton parrots, spears and other little things which would be tedious to describe, and gave them away for any thing that was given to them. I examined them closely and tried to ascertain if there was any gold, and noticed that some carried a small piece of it hanging from a little hole in their nose, and by signs I was able to understand that by going to the south or going around the island to the southward, there was a king who had large gold vessels, and gold in abundance. I endeavored to persuade them to go there, and I afterwards saw that they had no wish to go. I determined to wait until tomorow evening, and then to sail for the southwest, for many of them told me that there was land to the south and to the southwest and to the northwest, and that those from the northwest came frequently to fight with them, and so go to the southwest to get gold and precious stones. This island is very large and very level and has very green trees, and abundance of water, and a very large lagoon in the middle, without any mountain, and all is covered with verdue, most pleasing to the eye; the people are remarkably gentle, and from the desire to get some of our things, and thinking that nothing will be given to them

que den algo y no lo tienen, toman lo que pueden y se echan luego á nadar; mas todo lo que tienen lo dan por cualquiera cosa que les den; que fasta los pedazos de las escudillas, y de las tazas de vidrio rotas rescataban, fasta que ví dar diez y seis ovillos de algodon por tres ceotis(¹) de Portugal, que es una blanca de Castilla, y en ellos habria mas de una arroba de algodon filado. Esto defendiera y no dejára tomar á nadie, salvo que yo lo mandára tomar todo para V. A. si hobiera en cantidad. Aquí nace en esta isla, mas por el poco tiempo no pude dar así del todo fé, y tambien aquí nace el oro que traen colgado á la nariz; mas por no perder tiempo quiero ir á ver si puedo topar á la isla de Cipango(²). Agora como fue noche todos se fueron á tierra con sus almadias."

Domingo 14 de Octubre.

"En amaneciendo mandé aderezar el batel de la nao y las barcas de las carabelas, y fue al luengo de la isla, en el camino del Nornordeste, para ver la otra parte, que era de la otra parte del Leste que habia, y tambien para ver las poblaciones, y vide luego dos ó tres y la gente, que venian todos á la playa llamándonos y dando gracias á Dios; los unos nos traian agua, otros otras cosas de comer; otros, cuando veian que yo no curaba de ir á tierra, se echaban á la mar nadando y venian, y entendiamos que nos preguntaban si eramos venidos del cielo; y vino uno viejo en el batel dentro, y otros á voces grandes llamaban todos hombres y mugeres: venid á ver los hombres que vinieron del cielo: traedles de comer y de beber. Vinieron muchos y muchas mugeres, cada uno con algo, dando gracias á Dios, echándose al suelo, y levantaban las manos al cielo, y despues á voces nos llamaban que fuésemos á tierra: mas yo temia de ver una grande restinga de piedras que cerca toda aquella isla al rededor, y entre medias queda hondo y puerto para cuantas naos hay en toda la cristiandad, y la entrada dello muy angosta. Es verdad que dentro desta cinta

(¹) Por Ceuti ó cepti, moneda de Ceuta que corria en Portugal.

(²) Marco Polo en el cap. cvi de la relacion de su viage asegura haber visto esta isla, de la cual hace una larga descripcion, y añade que estaba situada en alta mar, á distancia de 1500 millas del continente de la India. El Dr. Robertson dice que probablemente es el Japon. Recherches hist. sur l'Inde ancienne, sec. 3.

unless they give some thing, and having nothing they take what they can and swim off [to the ship]; but all that they have they give for any thing that is offered to them; so that they bought even pieces of crockery, and pieces of broken glass, and I saw sixteen balls of cotton given for three ceotis(¹) of Portugal, which is equivalent to a blanca of Castile, and in them there must have been more than one arroba(²) of spun cotton. I forbad this and allowed no one to take any unless I ordered it to be taken for your Highnesses should it be found in abundance. It grows in the island, although on account of the shortness of time I could not assert it positively, and likewise the gold which they carry hanging in their noses is found here; but in order to lose no time I am now going to try if I can find the island of Cipango. At this moment it is dark and all went on shore in their canoes."

Sunday October 14.

"At dawn I ordered the boat of the ship and the boats of the Caravels to be got ready, and went along the island, in a north-northeasterly direction, to see the other side, which was on the other side of the east, and also to see the villages, and soon saw two or three and their inhabitants, coming to the shore calling us and praising God; some brought us water, some eatables; others, when they saw that I did not care to go on shore, plunged into the sea swimming and came, and we understood that they asked us if we had come down from heaven; and one old man got into the boat, while others in a loud voice called both men and women saying: come and see the men from heaven: bring them food and drink. A crowd of men and many women came, each bringing something, giving thanks to God, throwing themselves down, and lifting their hands to heaven, and entreating or beseeching us to land there: but I was afraid of a reef of rocks which entirely surrounds that island, although there is within it depth enough and ample harbor for all the vessels of christendom, but the entrance is very narrow. It is true that the interior of that belt contains some rocks, but the sea is there as still as the water in a well. And in order to see all this I moved this morning, that I might

(¹) Copper coin of the value of half a maravedi—Spanish Dictionary.

(²) Equal to 25.353145 pounds. Modern Metrology: Lowis D'A. Jackson: London, p. 310.

hay algunas bajas, mas la mar no se mueve mas que dentro en un pozo. Y para ver todo esto me moví esta mañana, porque supiese dar de todo relacion á vuestras Altezas, y tambien á donde pudiera hacer fortaleza, y vide un pedazo de tierra que se hace como isla, aunque no lo es, en que habia seis casas, el cual se pudiera atajar en dos dias por isla; aunque yo no veo ser necesario, porque esta gente es muy simplice en armas, como verán vuestras Altezas de siete que yo hice tomar para le llevar y deprender nuestra fabla y volvellos, salvo que vuestras Altezas cuando mandaren puedenlos todos llevar á Castilla, ó tenellos en la misma isla captivos, porque con cincuenta hombres los terná todos sojuzgados, y les hará hacer todo lo que quisiere; y despues junto con la dicha isleta estan huertas de árboles las mas hermosas que yo ví, ó tan verdes y con sus hojas como las de Castilla en el mes de Abril y de Mayo, y mucha agua. Yo miré todo aquel puerto, y despues me volví á la nao y dí la vela, y vide tantas islas que yo no sabia determinarme á cual iria primero, y aquellos hombres que yo tenia tomado me decian por señas que eran tantas y tantas que no habia número, y anombraron por su nombre mas de ciento[1]. Por ende yo miré por la mas grande[2], y aquella determiné andar, y así hago y será lejos desta de *San Salvador*, cinco leguas y las otras dellas mas, dellas menos: todas son muy llanas, sin montañas y muy fértiles, y todas pobladas, y se hacen guerra la una á la otra, aunque estos son muy simplices y muy lindos cuerpos de hombres.".

Lunes 15 de Octubre.

,, Habia temporejado esta noche con temor de no llegar á tierra á sorgir antes de la mañana por no saber si la costa era limpia de bajas, y en amaneciendo cargar velas. Y como la isla fuese mas lejos de cinco leguas, antes será siete, y la marea me detuvo, seria medio dia cuando llegué á la dicha isla, y falló que aquella haz, ques de la parte de la isla de *San Salvador*, se corre Norte Sur, y hay en ella cinco leguas, y la otra que yo seguí se corria Leste Oueste, y hay en ella mas de diez leguas. Y como desta isla vide otra mayor al Oueste,

[1] La multitud de estas islas indica que deben ser las que forman *los Caicos*, *las Inaguas chica y grande*, *Mariguana*, y demas que se hallan al Oeste.

[2] Esta isla grande debe ser la que llaman *Gran Caico*, y dista de la primera 6½ leguas.

give an account of everything to your Highnesses, and also to see where a fort could be built, and found a piece of land like an island, although it is not one, with six houses on it, which in two days could easily be cut off and converted into an island; such a work however is not necessary in my opinion, because the people are totally unacquainted with arms, as your Highnesses will see by observing the seven whom I have caused to be taken in order to carry them to Castile to be taught our language, and to return them unless your Highnesses when they shall send orders may take them all to Castile, or keep them in the same island as captives, for with fifty men all can be kept in subjection, and made to do whatever you desire; and near by the said little island there are orchards of trees the most beautiful that I have seen, with leaves as fresh and green as those of Castile in April and May, and much water. I observed all that harbor, and afterwards I returned to the ship and set sail, and saw so many islands that I could not decide to which one I should go first, and the men I had taken told me by signs that they were innumerable, and named more than one hundred of them. In consequence I looked for the largest one and determined to make for it, and I am so doing, and it is probably distant five leagues from this of *San Salvador*, the others some more, some less : all are very level, without mountains and of great fertility, and all are inhabited, and they make war upon each other, although these are very simple hearted and very finely formed men."

Monday October 15th.

"I had been standing off and on this night fearing to approach the shore for anchorage before morning not knowing whether the coast would be clear of shoals, and intending to clew up at dawn. And as the island was over five leagues distant, rather seven, and the tide detained me, it was about noon when I reached the said island, and I found that that side, which is towards the island of *San Salvador*, runs north [and] south, and is five leagues in length, and the other which I followed ran east [and] west, and contains over ten leagues. And as from this island I saw another larger one to the west, I clewed up the sails for I had gone all that day until night, because I could not yet have gone to the western cape,

cargué las velas por andar todo aquel dia fasta la noche, porque aun no pudiera haber andado al cabo del Oeste, á la cual puse nombre la *isla de Santa María de la Concepcion*([1]), y cuasi al poner del sol sorgí accrca del dicho cabo por saber si habia allí oro, porque estos que yo habia hecho tomar en la isla de S. Salvador me decian que ahí traian manillas de oro muy grandes á las piernas y á los brazos. Yo bien creí que todo lo que decian era burla para se fugir. Con todo, mi voluntad era de no pasar por ninguna isla de que no tomase posesion, puesto que tomado de una se puede decir de todas; y sorgí é estuve hasta hoy Martes que en amaneciendo fuí á tierra con las barcas armadas, y salí, y ellos que eran muchos así desnudos, y de la misma condicion de la otra isla de San Salvador, nos dejaron ir por la isla y nos daban lo que les pedia. Y porque el viento cargaba á la traviesa Sueste no me quiso detener y partí para la mao, y una almadia grande estaba abordo de la carabela Niña, y uno de los hombres de la isla de San Salvador, que en ella era, se echó á la mar y se fue en ella, y la noche de antes á medio echado el otro([2])   y fue atrás la almadia, la cual fugió que jamas fue barca que le pudiese alcanzar, puesto que le teniamos grande avante. Con todo dió en tierra, y dejaron la almadia, y alguno de los de mi compañía salieron en tierra tras ellos, y todos fugeron como gallinas, y la almadia que habian dejado la llevamos abordo de la carabela Niña, adonde ya de otro cabo venia otra almadia pequeña con un hombre que venia á rescatar un ovillo de algodon, y se echaron algunos marineros á la mar porque él no queria entrar en la carabela, y le tomaron; y yo que estaba á la popa de la mao, que vide todo, envié por él, y le dí un bonete colorado y unas cuentas de vidrio verdes pequeñas que le puse al brazo, y dos cascabeles que le puse á las orejas, y le mandé volver su almadia que tambien tenia en la barca, y le envié á tierra; y dí luego la vela para ir á la otra isla grande que yo via al Oeste, y mandé largar tambien la otra almadia que traia la carabela Niña por popa, y vide des-

to which([1]) **I** gave the name of the *island of Santa Maria de la Concepcion*, and about sunset I anchored near said cape in order to learn whether there was gold there, because the men whom I had caused to be taken from San Salvador told me that they there were very large rings of gold on their legs and arms. I well suspected that all they said was deceptive in order to get away from me. Nevertheless, it was my desire not to pass any island without taking possession of it, as one taken possession of the same may be said of all; and I anchored and remained until to day tuesday when at dawn I went on shore with the boats armed, and got out, and they who were many in number naked, and of the same disposition as those of the other island of San Salvador, allowed us to go over the island and gave us whatever we asked for. And because the wind was increasing across south east([2]) I did not like to stay longer so I returned to the ship, and a large canoe was alongside the caravel Niña, and one of the men of the island of San Salvador, who was in it, jumped overboard and escaped in it, and in the middle of the preceding night the other([3])   and he went after the canoe, which fled so swiftly that there was never a boat that could overtake it, although we had a long start. Nevertheless it reached the land, and they left the canoe, and some of my men went on shore after them, and they all ran like hens, and the canoe they had left we took on board the caravel Niña, to which from another quarter another small canoe was coming with a man who came to barter a ball of cotton, and as he refused to go on board the caravel, some sailors plunged into the sea and took him; and

---

([1]) Esta parece ser la que hoy se llama *Caico del Norte;* aunque con el nombre de *Santa María de la Concepcion* comprendió todo el grupo de las islas inmediatas que se llaman *los Caicos,* como se nota mas adelante en el dia 16 de Octubre.

([2]) Con la ininteligible escritura de esta palabra en el original, y el vacío ó hueco que sigue, queda obscuro el sentido del período. Acaso quiso decir: *y la noche de antes al medio se echó el otro á nado, y fue atrás la almadia, &c.*

([1]) The pronoun, which, is feminine in Spanish and cannot relate to cape which is masculine. It is therefore manifest that Columbus applied the name to the whole island.—H. L. T., translator.

([2]) The phrase in the Spanish text is—*El viento cargaba á la traviesa Sueste.* I find so much diversity in regard to the meaning of *á la traviesa,* that I venture a nautical explanation, provided he was where I put him on the forenoon of the 16th of October—N. W. end of Crooked Island.—Here the flood tide ran east, on the 16th, from 9ʰ a. m. to 3ʰ 12ᵐ p. m.—see p. 47—His ships were riding at single anchor, to a windward tide, with their heads to the westward; but as the *south east wind increased* there was the risk of "breaking shear," which the Admiral observed from the shore; hence his anxiety to be off.

([3]) On account of the illegible writing of this word in the original and the blank space that follows, the meaning of the sentence remains in obscurity. Perhaps he meant: *and in the middle of the preceding night the other swam off, and went behind the canoe, &c.* Casas.

pues en tierra al tiempo de la llegada del otro á quien yo habia dado las cosas susodichas, y no le habia querido tomar el ovillo de algodon puesto quel me lo queria dar; y todos los otros se llegaron á él, y tenia á gran maravilla ó bien le pareció que eramos buena gente, y que el otro que se habia fugido nos habia hecho algun daño y que por esto lo llevábamos, y á esta razon usé esto con él de le mandar alargar, y le dí las dichas cosas porque nos tuviesen en esta estima, porque otra vez cuando vuestras Altezas aquí tornen á enviar no hagan mala compañía; y todo lo que yo le dí no valia cuatro maravedís. Y así partí, que serian las diez horas, con el viento Sueste y tocaba de Sur para pasar á estotra isla, la cual es grandísima, y adonde todos estos hombres que yo traigo de la de San Salvador hacen señas que hay muy mucho oro, y que lo traen en los brazos en manillas, y á las piernas, y á las orejas, y al nariz, y al pescuezo. Y habia de esta isla de Santa María á esta otra nueve leguas Leste Oueste, y se corre toda esta parte de la isla Norueste Sueste, y se parece que bien habria en esta costa mas de veinte y ocho leguas(1) en esta faz, y es muy llana sin montaña ninguna, así como aquellas de San Salvador y de Santa María, y todas playas sin roquedos, salvo que á todas hay algunas peñas acerca de tierra debajo del agua, por donde es menester abrir el ojo cuando se quiere surgir ó no surgir mucho acerca de tierra, aunque las aguas son siempre muy claras y se ve el fondo. Y desviado de tierra dos tiros de lombarda hay en todas estas Islas tanto fondo que no se puede llegar á él. Son estas Islas muy verdes y fértiles, y de aires muy dulces, y puede haber muchas cosas que yo no sé, porque no me quiero detener por calar y andar muchas Islas para fallar oro. Y pues estas dan así estas señas que lo traen á los brazos y á las piernas, y es oro porque les amostré algunos pedazos del que yo tengo, no puedo errar con el ayuda de nuestro Señor que yo no le falle adonde nace. Y estando á medio golfo destas dos islas es de saber de aquella de Santa María y de esta grande, á la cual pongo nombre la *Fernandina*(2), fallé un hombre solo en una almadia que se pasaba de la isla de Santa María á la Fernandina, y traia un poco de su pan, que seria tanto como el' puño, y una calabaza de agua, y un pedazo de tierra bermeja

(1) Son solo 19 leguas.
(2) Conócese ahora con el nombre de *Inagua chica.*

I who from the poop of my ship saw all, sent for him, and I gave him a red cap put around his arm a string of small green glass beads, and two little bells on his cars, and ordered that his canoe which they also had on board of the vessel, should be returned to him, and thus I sent him on shore; and soon after I set sail for the other large island that appeared at the west, and I ordered that the other canoe that the Niña had astern should be turned adrift, when the man to whom I made the indicated presents and from whom I had refused the ball of cotton he offered to me reached the land; he was as I saw immediately surrounded by those on shore, and he thought it a great wonder and thought that we were good people, and that the other man who had fled had probably been kept by us in consequence of some injury done us, and that was the reason why I gave him presents and ordered his release, my aim being to win thus the respect and esteem of all, and avoid their enmity to the future expeditions your Highnesses may send; and yet all I gave him was not worth four maravedis. And so I left, at about ten o'clock, with a south east wind inclining to the south for the other island, a very large one, where the San Salvador men I have with me assert by signs there exists much gold, and that they wear it in rings around their arms, and legs, and in their ears, and noses, and around their necks. And from this island of Santa Maria to the other one there are nine leagues east [and] west, and all this portion of the island runs north west [and] south east, and it appears that there are on this coast more than twenty eight leagues it is even, and devoid of mountains, like those of San Salvador and Santa María, and all its shores are free from reefs, except some sunken rocks near the land which require great watchfulness when one wants to anchor or makes it prudent to anchor some distance from land, although the water is remarkably limpid and the bottom can be seen. And at the distance of two lombard shots there is in all these islands so much bottom that it cannot be reached. These islands are very green and fertile, and have a balmy atmosphere, they probably contain many things which I do not know of, for I do not wish to stop but to reconnoitre many islands in search of gold. And since these thus give these signs that they wear it on their arms and legs, and it is real gold for I showed them some pieces of that which I have, I cannot fail God helping find-

18

hecha en polvo y despues amasada, y unas hojas secas que debe ser cosa muy apreciada entre ellos, porque ya me trujeron en San Salvador dellas en presente, y traia un cestillo á su guisa en que tenia un ramalejo de cuentecillas de vidrio y dos blancas, por las cuales conoscí qnel venia de la isla de San Salvador, y habia pasado á aquella de Santa María, y se pasaba á la Fernandina, el cual se llegó á la nao; yo le hice entrar, que así lo demandaba él, y le hice poner su almadia en la nao, y guardar todo lo que él traia; y le mandé dar de comer pan y miel, y de beber; y así le pasaré á la Fernandina, y le daré todo lo suyo, porque dé buenas nuevas de nos para á nuestro Señor aplaciendo, cuando vuestras Altezas envien acá, que aquellos que vinieren resciban honra, y nos den de todo lo que hubiere."

Martes 16 de Octubre.

,, Partí de las *islas de Santa María de la Concepcion,* que seria ya cerca del medio dia, para la *isla Fernandina,* la cual amuestra ser grandísima al Oueste, y navegué todo aquel dia con calmeria; no pude llegar á tiempo de poder ver el fondo para surgir en limpio, porque es en esto mucho de haber gran diligencia por no perder las anclas; y así temporicé toda esta noche hasta el dia que vine á una poblacion, adonde yo surgí, ó adonde habia venido aquel hombre que yo hallé ayer en aquella almadia á medio golfo, el cual habia dado tantas buenas nuevas de nos que toda esta noche no faltó almadias abordo de la nao, que nos traian agua y de lo que tenian. Yo á cada uno le mandaba dar algo, es á saber algunas cuentecillas, diez ó doce dellas de vidrio en un filo, y algunas sonajas de laton destas que valen en Castilla un marvedí cada una, y algunas agujetas, de que todo tenian en grandísima excelencia, y tambien los mandaba dar para que comiesen cuando venian en la nao miel de azúcar; y despues á horas de tercia envié el batel de la nao en tierra por agua, y ellos de muy buena gana le enseñaban á mi gente adonde estaba el agua, y ellos mismos traian

ing the place whence it is procured. And being in the gulf midway between these two islands namely that of Santa Maria and this large one, to which I give the name of la *Fernandina,* I found a man who was going from the island of Santa Maria to la Fernandina, he had a small piece of his bread, about the size of one's fist, a calabash of water, a lump of red earth reduced to powder and afterwards kneaded, and some dry leaves highly prized no doubt among them, for those of San Salvador offered some to me as a present,[1] and he carried a little basket in their fashion in which he had a small string of glass beads and two blancas, by which I knew that he came from the island of San Salvador, had passed to Santa Maria, and was now going to la Fernandina, and he came to the ship; I had him taken on board as he desired, and ordered that his canoe and all that he had, should be kept in the ship; and had him treated with bread honey, and drink; and I will take him to la Fernandina, giving him back what he has brought, in order that he may give good news concerning us so that God willing, when your Highnesses shall send here, those who shall come may receive honor, and that they may give us of all that they have."

Tuesday October 16th.

"About noon I left the *islands of Santa Maria de la Concepcion* for the *island of Fernandina,* which appears to be very large to the west, and I sailed all that day with calm weather; I could not arrive in time to see the bottom in order to get a clear anchorage, a thing requiring the greatest care in order not to lose the anchors; in consequence I waited until daylight when I anchored near a village, the man whom I found yesterday in his canoe in the gulf had come to that village, and so favorable was the account he had given of us that to night they have been constantly coming to the ship in their canoes, bringing us water and everything they have. I caused some things to be given to every one, such as small beads, ten or twelve of them of glass on a string, some brass [tin?] rattles like those that in Castile can be had for

[1] This was probably tobacco. When at Port Nuevitas del Principe, Cuba, November 6th, the two messengers he sent into the country returned and reported, among other things, that the natives, men and women, fumigated themselves by inhaling smoke from tubes—*tabacos*—made of dried leaves. This is the first record of smoking cigars. See Navarrete, 1st edition, p. 51. Note by Las Casas.

los barriles llenos al batel, y se folgaban mucho de nos hacer placer. Esta isla es grandísima y tengo determinado de la rodear, porque segun puedo entender en ella, ó cerca della, hay mina de oro. Esta isla está desviada de la de Santa María ocho leguas cuasi Leste Oueste; y este cabo adonde yo vine, y toda esta costa se corre Nornorueste y Sursueste, y vide bien veinte leguas de ella, mas ahí no acababa. Agora escribiendo esto dí la vela con el viento Sur para pujar á rodear toda la isla, y trabajar hasta que halle *Samaot*, que es la isla ó ciudad adonde es el oro, que así lo dicen todos estos que aquí vienen en la nao, y nos lo decian los de la isla de San Salvador y de Santa María. Esta gente es semejante á aquella de las dichas islas, y una fabla y unas costumbres, salvo questos ya me parecen algun tanto mas doméstica gente, y de tracto, y mas sotiles, porque veo que han traido algodon aquí á la nao y otras cositas que saben mejor refertar(¹) el pagamento que no hacian los otros; y aun en esta isla vide paños de algodón fechos como mantillos, y la gente mas dispuesta, y las mugeres traen por delante su cuerpo una cosita de algodon que escasamente les cobija su natura. Ella es isla muy verde y llana y fertilísima, y no pongo duda que todo el año siembran panizo y cogen, y así todas otras cosas; y vide muchos árboles muy disformes de los nuestros, y dellos muchos que tenian los ramos de muchas maneras y todo en un pie, y un ramito es de una manera y otro de otra, y tan disforme que es la mayor maravilla del mundo cuanta es la diversidad de la una manera á la otra, verbi gracia, un ramo tenia las fojas á manera de cañas y otro de manera de lentisco; y así en un solo árbol de cinco ó seis de estas maneras; y todos tan diversos: ni estos son enjeridos, porque se pueda decir que el enjerto lo hace, antes son por los montes, ni cura dellos esta gente. No le conozco secta ninguna, y creo que muy presto se tornarian cristianos, porque ellos son de muy buen entender. Aquí son los peces tan disformes de los nuestros ques maravilla. Hay algunos hechos como gallos de las mas finas colores del mundo, azules, amarillos, colorados y de todas colores, y otros pintados de mil maneras; y las colores son tan finas que no hay hombre que no se maraville y no tome gran descanso á verlos. Tambien hay ballenas: bestias en tierra no vide

(¹) Acaso *refertar* v. a. aut. contradecir, repugnar, resistir, reusar ó regatear.

one maravedí a piece, and some leather straps, all of which they held in the greatest estimation, and I also treated those who came to my ship with honey of sugar [molasses?]; and afterwards at nine o'clock a. m. I sent the ship's boat to the shore for water, and they willingly showed my men where the water was and they themselves brought the casks filled to the boat, and were very glad to be able to oblige us. This island is exceedingly large and I have determined to go around it, because as I can understand on it or near it, there is a mine of gold. This island lies at a distance from that of Santa Maria of eight leagues almost east [and] west; and this cape to which I have come, and all this coast, runs north-northwest and south-southeast, and I saw fully twenty leagues of it, but this was not the end. Soon after writing this I set sail with a south wind, intending to go around the whole island, and work until I should find *Samaot*, which is the island or city where the gold is, as all those say who have come with us in the ships, and as was before asserted by those of the island of San Salvador and Santa Maria. The people here are like those of the said islands, and speak the same language and have the same customs, but these look to me as somewhat more gentle, of better manners, and of keener intelligence, for I notice that in bartering cotton and other little things they know how to trade, which the others never did; and also on this island I saw cotton cloth made like mantles, and the people more intelligent, and the women wear in front a small piece of cotton stuff which scarcely covers what decency requires. The island is very green level and exceedingly fertile, and I doubt not that they sow and gather panizo(¹) and all other things, at all seasons of the year; and I saw many trees whose shape was very different from ours, and many of them which had branches of many kinds although growing from one trunk, and one branch is of one kind and another of another kind, and so different that the diversity of the kinds is the greatest wonder of the world, for instance, one branch had leaves like those of cane and another like those of a mastic; and thus on a single tree

(¹) Panicum—an ancient Latin name of the Italian millet *P. Italicum* (now *Setaria Italica*) thought to come from panis, bread; some species furnishing a kind of bread corn. *Gray's New Lessons and Manual of Botany.* Boston, 1868. p. 645.

ninguna de ninguna manera, salvo papagáyos y lagartos; un mozo me dijo que vido una grande culebra. Ovejas ni cabras ni otra ninguna bestia vide; aunque yo he estado aquí muy poco, que es medio dia, mas si las hobiese no pudiera errar de ver alguna. El cerco desta isla escribiré despues que yo la hobiere rodeado."

there were five or six of these kinds; and all so different: nor can it be said that they have been grafted, because those trees grow wild in the field, and nobody cares for them.[1] I know no sect among them, and as they are of very good understanding, they would in my opinion soon become Christians. The fishes here are so different from ours that it is a wonder. Some look like cocks of the finest colors in the world, blue, yellow, red and all colors, and others variegated in a thousand fashions; their different hues being so exquisite that nobody can contemplate them without wondering, and feeling great delight in seeing them.[2] There are also whales here: but on shore I saw no beasts whatever, save parrots and lizzards; a young man told me that he had seen a large snake. No sheep nor goats nor any other beast did I see; although I have only stopped half a day I could not fail in seeing some, should there be any. When I shall have sailed around this island I will describe its coast."

Miercoles 17 de Octubre.

„A medio dia partí de la poblacion adonde yo estaba surgido, y adonde tomé agua para ir rodear esta isla Fernandina, y el viento era Sudueste y Sur; y como mi voluntad fuese de seguir esta costa desta isla adonde yo estaba al Sueste, porque así se corre toda Nornorueste y Sursueste, y queria llevar el dicho camino de Sur y Sueste, porque aquella parte todos estos indios que traigo y otro de quien hobe señas en esta parte del Sur á la isla á que ellos llaman *Samoet*, adonde es el oro; y Martin Alonso Pinzon, capitan de la carabela Pinta, en la cual yo mandé á tres de estos indios, vino á mí y me dijo que uno dellos muy certificadamente le habia dado á entender que por la parte del Nornorueste muy mas presto arrodearia la isla. Yo vide que el viento no me ayudaba por el camino que yo queria llevar, y era bueno por el otro: dí la vela al Nornorueste, y cuando fue acerca del cabo de la isla, á dos leguas, hallé un muy maravilloso puerto con una boca, aunque dos bocas se le puede decir, porque tiene un isleo en medio, y son ambas muy angostas, y dentro muy ancho para cien[1] navíos si fuera fondo y limpio, y fondo al entrada: parecióme razon del ver bien y sondear, y así surgí fuera dél, y fui en él con todas las barcas de los navíos, y vimos que no habia fondo. Y porque pensé cuando yo

Wednesday October 17th.

At midday I left the village where I had anchored and taken in water, in order to sail around this island of Fernandina, the wind was southwest and south; and as my wish was to follow the coast of the island where I was to the southeast, because it all runs to the north-northwest and south-southeast, and I desired to take the said route of south and south-east, because that part all these Indians whom I have on board and another from whom I received signs in this part of the south on the island which they call *Samoet*, [is] where the gold is; and Martin Alonso Pinzon, captain of the caravel Pinta, into which I sent three of these Indians, came to me and said that one of them had very positively given him to understand that I should round the island much the quickest by the north-northwest. I saw that the wind was not favorable to my intended course,

---

(1) En el original dice *parecion;* pero es error conocido.

(1) The flora which Columbus saw has probably disappeared before the reckless firing and wasteful cultivation which characterizes the agriculture of the Bahamas. There are, however, now found there, besides the Epiphytes or air plants, many of a parasitic nature and two, Wild fig (*Ficus pedunculata*) and Scotch attorney (*clusca rosea*) which, springing from chance seed lodged in the branches of trees throw their roots to the ground and join their foliage as if belonging to the same trunk.

(2) This vivid description applies to the fishes which are now found on the Bahama banks.

le ví que era boca de algun rio habia mandado llevar barriles para tomar agua, y en tierra hallé unos ocho ó diez hombres que luego vinieron á nos, y nos amostraron ahí cerca la poblacion, adonde yo envié la gente por agua, una parte con armas otros con barriles, y así la tomaron; y porque era lejuelos me detuve por espacio de dos horas. En este tiempo anduve así por aquellos árboles, que era la cosa mas fermosa de ver que otra que se haya visto; veyendo tanta verdura en tanto grado como en el mes de Mayo en el Andalucía, y los árboles todos estan tan disformes de los nuestros como el dia de la noche; y así las frutas, y así las yerbas y las piedras y todas las cosas. Verdad es que algunos árboles eran de la naturaleza de otros que hay en Castilla, por ende habia muy gran diferencia, y los otros árboles de otras maneras eran tantos que no hay persona que lo pueda decir ni asemejar á otros de Castilla. La gente toda era una con los otros ya dichos, de las mismas condiciones, y así desnudos y de la misma estatura, y daban de lo que tenian por cualquiera cosa que les diesen; y aquí vide que unos mozos de los navíos les trocaron azagayas por unos pedazuelos de escudillas rotas y de vidrio, y los otros que fueron por el agua me dijeron como habian estado en sus casas, y que eran de dentro muy barridas y limpias, y sus camas y paramentos de cosa son como redes de algodon([1]): ellas las casas son todas á manera de alfaneques, y muy altas y buenas chimeneas([2]); mas no vide entre muchas poblaciones que yo vide ninguna que pasase de doce hasta quince casas. Aquí fallaron que las mugeres casadas traian bragas de algodon, las mozas no, sino salvo algunas que eran ya de edad de diez y ocho años. Y ahi habia perros mastines y branchetes, y ahí fallaron uno que habia al nariz un pedazo de oro que seria como la mitad de un castellano, en el cual vieron letras: reñí yo con ellos porque no se lo resgataron y dieron cuanto pedia, por ver que era y cuya esta moneda era; y ellos me respondieron que nunca se lo osó resgatar. Despues de tomada la agua volví á la nao, y dí la vela, y salí al Norueste tanto que yo descubrí toda aquella parte de la isla hasta la costa que se corre Leste Oueste, y despues todos estos indios tor-

([1]) Llámanse *Hamacas*.

([2]) Estas chimeneas no son para humeros, sino unas coronillas que tienen encima las casas de paja de los Indios. Por esto lo dice, puesto que dejan abierto por arriba algo para que salga el humo. *Casas.*

and was to the other: so I sailed to the north-north west, and when I was near the end of the island, two leagues off, I found a very marvellous port with an entrance, although it may be said that there are two entrances, because it has a rocky islet in the middle, and both are very narrow, but within it there is ample room for one hundred ships, if it had sufficient depth of water, and was clear, and had also a deep entrance: I thought it worth while to examine and sound it, and so I anchored outside of it, and went in with all the boats of the ships, and saw that there was not bottom. And because I thought when I saw it that it was the mouth of some river I had the casks sent on shore for water, and on shore I found eight or ten men who soon approached us, and showed us the village near by, to which I sent my men for water, some armed, and others with the casks, and thus they got it; and because it was rather far I was detained for the space of two hours. During this time I walked among those trees, which were the most beautiful things that were ever seen; so much verdure being visible and in as high a degree as in the month of May in Andalucia, and all these trees as different from ours as day is from night; the same was the case with the fruits, grass stones and all things. It is true that some trees were of the same family as others in Castile, however there was a very great difference, and the other trees of other kinds were so many that there is no person that can compare them to others in Castile. The people were all like those aforementioned, they have the same dispositions, go about naked and are of the same size, and gave of what they had for anything that was given to them; and here I saw that some young men of the vessels obtained spears from them for some little pieces of broken crockery and glass, the men I sent for water told us that the houses which they had entered were well swept and perfectly clean, and that their beds and coverings looked like cotton nets:([1]) the houses are like tents, very high and have good chimneys;([2]) but among the many villages which I saw none had over twelve or fifteen houses. Here they found that the married women wore cotton

([1]) Which they called Hamacas. *Navarrete.* This is the first mention of the hammock.

([2]) These are not chimneys for emitting smoke but are crowns on top of the straw huts, he called them chimneys because something is left open on top in order that the smoke may get out. *Casas.*

naron á decir que esta isla era mas pequeña que no la isla *Samoet*, y que seria bien volver átras por ser en ella mas presto. El viento allí luego mas calmó y comenzó á ventar Ouesnorueste, el cual era contrario para donde habiamos venido, y así tomé la vuelta y navegué toda esta noche pasada al Lestesueste, y cuando al Leste todo y cuando al Sueste; y esto para apartarme de la tierra porque hacia muy gran cerrazon y el tiempo muy cargado: el era poco y no me dejó llegar á tierra á surgir. Así que esta noche llovió muy fuerte despues de media noche hasta cuasi el dia, y aun está nublado para llover; y nos al cabo de la isla de la parte del Sueste adonde espero surgir fasta que aclarezca para ver las otras islas adonde tengo de ir; y así todos estos dias despues que en estas Indias estoy ha llovido poco ó mucho. Crean vuestras Altezas que es esta tierra la mejor é mas fertil, y temperada, y llana, y buena que haya en el mundo."

breeches, the young girls not, except a few who were already of the age of eighteen years. And they had there dogs mastines([1]) and branchetes,([2]) and here they found one wearing in his nose a piece of gold of the size of half a castillano,([3]) on which they saw letters: I scolded them for not having got it by giving whatever he asked, in order to see what it was and if coin whose coin it was; but they answered that he did not dare to barter it. After getting in water I returned to the ship, and set sail, and sailed to the northwest until I discovered all that part of the island as far as the coast which runs east [and] west, and afterwards these Indians again said that this island was smaller than the island of *Samoet*, and that it would be well to go back as we would thus reach it sooner. The wind then ceased and then sprang up from west-northwest, which was contrary to our course, and so I turned around and sailed all the past night to the east-southeast, and sometimes wholly east, and sometimes to the southeast; this I did in order to keep off the land for the atmosphere was very misty and the weather threatening: it [the wind] was light and did not permit me to reach the land in order to anchor. So that this night it rained very hard after midnight until almost day, and is still cloudy in order to rain; and we [are] at the southeast cape of the island where I hope to anchor until it gets clear in order to see the other islands where I have to go; ever since I came to these Indies it has been raining much or little. I beg your Highnesses to believe however that this land is the richest, the mildest in temperature, and the most level and wholesome in the world."

Jueves 18 de Octubre.

„Despues que aclareció seguí el viento, y fuí en derredor de la isla cuanto pude, y surgí al tiempo que ya no era de navegar; mas no fuí en tierra, y en amaneciendo dí la vela."

Thursday October 18th.

"After it cleared up I followed the wind, and went around the island as much as I could, and I anchored when it was no longer possible to sail; but I did not go on shore, and at dawn I set sail."

Viernes 19 de Octubre.

„En amaneciendo levanté las anclas y envié la carabela Pinta al Leste y Sueste y la carabela Niña al Sursueste, y yo con la nao fuí al Sueste, y dado orden que llevasen aquella vuelta fasta medio dia, y despues que ambas se mudasen las derrotas y se recogieran para mí; y luego antes que andásemos tres horas vimos

Friday, October 19th.

"At dawn I weighed anchor and sent the caravel Pinta to the east and southeast and the caravel Niña to the south-southeast, and I

([1]) Mastines—mastiff.
([2]) Branchetes—probably a scenting dog.
([3]) One castillano of gold equal to $1.66\frac{2}{3}$. *Irving's Columbus*, revised edition. 1848. Note. Vol. II, p. 49.

23

una isla al Leste, sobre la cual descargamos, y llegamos á ella todos tres navíos antes de medio dia á la punta del Norte, adonde hace un isleo y una restinga de piedra fuera de él al Norte, y otro entre él y la isla grande; la cual auombraron estos hombres de *San Salvador*, que yo traigo, la isla *Saometo*, á la cual puse nombre la *Isabela*(¹). El viento era Norte, y quedaba el dicho isleo en derrota de la isla *Fernandina*, de adonde yo habia partido Leste oueste, y se corria despues la costa desde el isleo al Oueste, y habia en ella doce leguas fasta un cabo, á quien yo llamé el *Cabo hermoso*, que es de la parte del Oueste; y así es fermoso, redondo y muy fondo, sin bajas fuera de él, y al comienzo es de piedra y bajo, y mas adentro es playa de arena como cuasi la dicha costa es, y ahí surgí esta noche Viernes hasta la mañana. Esta costa toda, y la parte de la isla que yo ví, es toda cuasi playa, y la isla mas fermosa cosa que yo ví; que si las otras son muy hermosas, esta es mas: es de muchos árboles y muy verdes, y muy grandes; y esta tierra es mas alta que las otras islas falladas, y en ella algun altillo, no que se le pueda llamar montaña, mas cosa que afermosea lo otro, y parece de muchas agnas allá al medio de la isla; de esta parte al Nordeste hace una grande angla, y ha muchos arboledos, y muy espesos y muy grandes. Yo quise ir á surgir en ella para salir á tierra, y ver tanta fermosura; mas era el fondo bajo y no podia surgir salvo largo de tierra, y el viento era muy bueno para venir á este cabo, adonde yo surgí agora, al cual puse nombre *Cabo Fermoso*, porque así lo es; y así no surgí en aquella angla, y aun porque vide este cabo de allá tan verde y tan fermoso, así como todas las otras cosas y tierras destas islas que yo no sé adonde me vaya primero, ni me sé cansar los ojos de ver tan fermosas verduras y tan diversas de las nuestras, y aun creo que ha en ellas muchas yerbas y muchos árboles, que valen mucho en España para tinturas y para medicinas de especería, mas yo no los cognozco, de que llevo grande pena. Y llegando yo aquí á este cabo vino el olor tan bueno y suave de flores ó árboles de la tierra que era la cosa mas dulce del mundo. De mañaua antes que yo de aquí vaya iré en tierra á ver que es aquí en el cabo; no es la poblacion salvo allá mas adentro adonde di-

(¹) Parece que la *Isabela* corresponde á la isla que ahora se conoce con el nombre de *Inagua grande*, y los indios llamaban *Saometo*.

with the ship went to the southeast, having given orders that they should keep that course until midday, and then that both should change their course and return to me; and then before we had gone three hours we saw an island to the east, to which we directed our course, and all the three vessels reached it before midday at its northern extremity, where there is a rocky islet and a ridge of rocks outside it to the north, and another between it and the large island; which the men of *San Salvador*, that I brought with me, called *Saometo*, to which I gave the name of la *Isabela*. The wind was north, and the said islet lay from the island of *Fernandina*, whence I had come east [and] west, and the coast afterwards ran from the rocky islet to the westward, and there was in it twelve leagues as far as a cape, which I called *Cape Beautiful*, which is in the west; and so it is beautiful, round and [the water?] very deep and free from shoals, at first it is rocky and low, but farther in it is a sandy beach as it is along most of the coast, and it is here that I anchored to-night Friday, anchored until morning. This coast all, and the part of the island that I saw, is nearly all a beach, and the island the most beautiful thing I have seen; if the others are very beautiful this is still more so: it has many trees very green, and very large; and this land is higher than that of the other islands I have discovered, although it cannot be called mountainous, yet gentle hills enhance with their contrasts the beauty of the plain, and there appears to be much water in the middle of the island; northeast of this cape there is an extensive promontory, and there are many groves, very thick and very large. I wished to anchor off it in order to land, and visit so handsome a spot; but it was shallow and I could not anchor except far from land, and the wind was very favorble to come to this cape, where I have now anchored, and which I have called *Cape Beautiful*, because it is so; and so I did not anchor off that promontory, because I saw this cape so green and so beautiful, as are all the other things and lands of these islands so that I do not know to which to go first, nor do my eyes grow tired with looking at such beautiful verdure, so different from our own, and I even believe that among it there are many grasses or herbs, and many trees which would be of great value in Spain for dyes and medicines, but I do not know them, which I greatly regret. And

24

cen estos hombres que yo traigo, que está el Rey y que trae mucho oro; y yo de mañana quiero ir tanto avante que halle la poblacion, y vea ó haya lengua con este Rey, que segun estos dan las señas él señorea todas estas islas comarcanas, y va vestido, y trae sobre sí mucho oro; aunque no doy mucha fé á sus decires, así por no los entender yo bien, como en cognoscer quellos son tan pobres de oro que cualquiera poco que este Rey traiga les parece á ellos mucho. Esto á quien yo digo *Cabo Fermoso* creo que es isla apartada de *Saometo*, y aun hay ya otra entremedias pequeña: yo no curo así de ver tanto por menudo, porque no lo podia facer en cincuenta años, porque quiero ver y descubrir lo mas que yo pudiere para volver á vuestras Altezas, á nuestro Señor aplaciendo, en Abril. Verdad es que fallando adonde haya oro ó especería en cantidad me deterné fasta que yo haya dello cuanto pudiere; y por esto no fago sino andar para ver de topar en ello.''

Sabado 20 de Octubre.

„Hoy al sol salido levanté las anclas de donde yo estaba con la nao surgido en esta isla de *Saometó* al cabo del Sudueste, adonde yo puse nombre el *Cabo de la Laguna* y á la isla la *Isabela*, para navegar al Nordeste y al Leste de la parte del Sueste y Sur, adonde entendí de estos hombres que yo traigo que era la poblacion y el Rey de ella; y fallé todo tan bajo el fondo que no pude entrar ni navegar á ello, y vide que siguiendo el camino del Sudueste era muy gran rodeo, y por esto determiné de me volver por el camino que yo habia traido del Nornordeste de la parte del Oueste, y rodear esta isla para[(1)] el viento me fue tan escaso que yo no nunca pude haber la tierra al longo de la costa salvo en la noche; y por ques peligro[(2)] surgir en estas islas, salvo en el dia que se vea con el ojo adonde se echa el ancla, porque es todo manchas, una de limpio y otra de nou, yo me

(1) Igual vacio en el original. Parece falta *reconocerla*.
(2) Así el original: parece ha de decir *peligroso*.

when I reached this cape the odor came so good and sweet from flowers or trees on the land that it was the sweetest thing in the world. To-morrow before leaving here I will go on shore to see what there is on this cape; there is no population except farther inland where according to the information received from these men whom I have on board, their king lives and has much gold; I intend to proceed to-morrow until I find the population, and see or converse with this king, who, according to the signs made by these men is master of all these neighboring islands, and goes clothed, and wears much gold on his person; although I place little confidence in their assertions, both because I do not understand well and because I see that they are so poor in gold that any small quantity worn by this King would seem to them to be a great deal. I believe that this *Cape Beautiful* is a separate island from *Saometo*, and even that there is another small one between: for that reason I do not care to examine so much in detail, because I could not do it in fifty years, because I desire to see and discover the most that I can, in order to return to your Highnesses, God willing, in April. It is true that I will stop wherever I may find gold or spices in large quantities and get as much of each as possible; I am constantly sailing in order to find some.''

Saturday, October 20th.

"At sunrise I weighed anchor from the place where I was with the vessel anchored at this island of *Saometo* at the southwest cape, which I named the *Cape of the Lagoon* and I called the island la *Isabela*, in order to sail to the northeast and to the east towards the southeast and south, where I understood from these men whom I have with me that the population and their king were; and so I found the bottom so shallow that I could not enter or sail to it, and I saw that by following a southwestern route it would be a long way around, and consequently I determined to return by the course I had come from the north-northeast toward the west, and to go around this island in order[(1)] The wind, however, was so scant that I was never able to have the land along the coast except at night; and because it is dangerous to anchor among these islands, save in the day-time when

(1) A blank in the original, probably to reconnoiter it. Navarrete.

puse á temporejar á la vela toda esta noche del Domingo. Las carabelas surgieron porque se hallaron en tierra temprano, y pensaron que á sus señas, que eran costumbradas de hacer, iria á surgir; mas no quise."

Domingo 21 de Octubre.

„A las diez horas llegué aquí á este cabo del isleo, y surgí y asímismo las carabelas; y despues de haber comido fui en tierra, adonde aquí no habia otra poblacion que una casa, en la cual no fallé á nadie que creo que con temor se habiau fugido porque en ella estaban todos sus aderezos de casa. Yo no les dejé tocar nada, salvo que me salí con estos capitanes y gente á ver la isla; que si las otras ya vistas son muy fermosas y verdes y fértiles, esta es mucho mas y de grandes arboledos y muy verdes. Aquí es unas grandes lagunas, y sobre ellas y á la rueda es el arboledo en maravilla, y aquí y en toda la isla son todos verdes y las yerbas como en el Abril en el Andalucía; y el cantar de los pajaritos que parece que el hombre nunca se querria partir de aquí, y las manadas de los papagayos que ascurecen el sol; y aves y pajaritos de tantas maneras y tan diversas de las nuestras que es maravilla; y despues ha árboles de mil maneras, y todos de su manera fruto, y todos huelen que es maravilla, que yo estoy el mas penado del mundo de no los cognoscer, porque soy bien cierto que todos son cosa de valía, y de ellos traigo la demuestra, y asimismo de las yerbas. Andando así eu cerco de una destas lagunas vide una sierpe(¹), la cual matamos y traigo el cuero á vuestras Altezas. Ella como nos vido se echó en la laguna, y nos la seguimos dentro, porque no era muy fonda, fasta que con lanzas la matamos; es de siete palmos en largo; creo que destas semejantes hay aquí en esta laguna muchas. Aquí cognoscí del liñaloe, y mañana he determinado de hacer traer á la nao diez quintales, porque me dicen que vale mucho. Tambien andando en busca de muy buena agua fuimos á una poblacion aquí cerca, adonde estoy surto media legua; y la gente, della como nos sintieron dieron todos á fugir, y dejaron las casas, y escondieron su ropa y lo que tenian por el monte; yo no dejé tomar nada ni la valia de un alfiler. Despues se llegaron á nos unos hombres dellos, y uno se llegó del todo aquí:

(¹) Yuana (*Iguana*) debió de ser esta. *Casas.*

App. 18——4

one sees with the eye where the anchor is cast, because it is all spots, one clean the other not, I stood off and on all this night of Sunday. The caravels anchored because they reached the land early, and thought that I would do the same at sight of their customary signals; but I did not wish to."

Sunday October 21st.

"At ten o'clock I arrived here at this end of the rocky islet, and I anchored as did the caravels; and after taking my dinner I went on shore, I found there only a house, in which I found no person and I believe that they had fled through fear because all their household goods were there. I did not allow them to touch anything, except that I went with the captains and men to see the island; if the others appeared beautiful, green, and fertile, this one with its majestic and luxuriant forests surpasses them all. Here are some large lagoons, and around them are the trees so that it is a marvel, and here and throughout the island they are all green and the grass is like it is in April in Andalucia; and the songs of the little birds so that it seems as if a man could never leave here, and the flocks of parrots which darken the sun; and birds and little birds of so many kinds and so different from ours that it is a marvel; and then there are trees of a thousand kinds, all bearing fruit of their own kinds, and all smell so that it is a marvel, so that I felt the greatest regret in the world not to know them, because I am very certain that they are all things of value, and I bring the samples of them, and also of the grasses. While going around one of these lagoons I saw a serpent,(¹) which we killed and I bring the skin to your Highnesses. When it saw us it plunged into the lagoon, and we followed it in, because it was not very deep, until we killed it with our lances; is of seven palmos(²) in length; I believe

---

(¹) This should be Ytuaa (Iguana) Casas.

(²) *Library of Universal Knowledge.* N. Y. 1881. Vol. XI, p. 225. Spanish Palmo Major is given as 8.3450 inches, English. Spanish Palmo Minor is given as 2.7817 inches, English. Either of these dimensions might apply to the Iguana, but in Columbus's letter to the King and Queen concerning his fourth voyage, Navarrete, p. 450, he wrote of a harbor in Veragna, "bien que á la entrada no tenio salvo diez *palmos* de fondo." He used the same word, "palmos," for the depth of the harbor's entrance, as he used for the length of the Iguana. As neither of the above dimensions can express his meaning in both quotations I leave the original word, palmos.

yo dí unos cascabeles y unas cuentecillas de vidrio, y quedó muy contento y muy alegre, y porque la amistad creciese mas y los requiriese algo le hice pedir agua, y ellos despues que fui en la nao vinieron luego á la playa con sus calabazas llenas y folgaron mucho de dárnosla, y yo les mandé dar otro ramalejo de cuentecillas de vidrio, y dijeron que de mañana vernian acá. Yo queria hinchir aquí toda la vasija de los navios de agua; por ende si el tiempo me da lugar luego me partiré á rodear esta isla fasta que yo haya lengua con este Rey, y ver si puedo haber dél el oro que oyo que trae, y despues partir para otra isla grande mucho, que creo que debe ser *Cipango*, segun las señas que me dan estos indios que yo traigo, á la cual ellos llaman *Colba*([1]), en la cual dicen que ha naos y marcantes muchos y muy grandes, y de esta isla otra que llaman *Bosio*([2]) que tambien dicen qués muy grande, y á las otras que son entremedio veré así de pasada, y segun yo fallare recaudo de oro ó especería determinaré lo que he de facer. Mas todavía tengo determinado de ir á la tierra firme y á la ciudad de *Guisay*, y dar las cartas de vuestras Altezas al *Gran Can*, y pedir respuesta y venir con ella."

Lunes 22 de Octubre.

„Toda esta noche y hoy estuve aquí aguardando si el Rey de aquí ó otras personas traerian oro ó otra cosa de sustancia, y vinieron muchos de esta gente, semejantes á los otros de las otras islas, así desnudos, y asi pintados dellos de blanco, dellos de colorado, dellos de prieto,

that there are many like this in this lagoon. Here I found the aloe tree, and as I have been told that it is very valuable I shall to-morrow, have ten quintals of it brought to the ship. While looking for good water we went to a village, distant half a league from my anchoring place; and the people fled at our approach, abandoning their houses, and hiding their wearing-apparel and what they had in the woods; and I did not allow them to take anything not even the value of a pin. Afterwards some of the men came to us, and one came quite up to us: I gave him some little bells and some glass beads, which satisfied and gladdened him very much, and in order that our friendship might increase and that I might ask something of them I asked for some water, which they after, I had gone on board the ship brought to the beach with their calabashes filled, and were very much pleased to give it to us, I had them presented with another small string of glass beads, and they said they would come the next day. I wanted to have all the casks in the ship supplied with water; consequently the weather permitting I shall sail at once in order to go until I get an interview with this king, to see if I can get from him the gold which I hear that he wears, and afterwards to sail for another very large island, which I think must be *Cipango*, according to the signs given me by those Indians whom I have on board, and which they called *Colba*,([1]) and where they say there are large ships and many merchants, and from it to another island named *Bosio*([2]) which they also say is very large, taking a passing notice of others between, and shaping my future conduct in accordance with the quantities of gold or spices that I may find. I have also decided to go to the mainland to the city of *Guisay*, present there the letters of your Highnesses to the *Grand Khan*, ask for an answer and come away with it."

Monday October 22d.

"All last night and to day I have remained here expecting the king or other persons to come with gold or some other valuable things, many of these people came naked, like those of the other islands, painted some white, some red, some black, and so on in many ways. They

---

([1]) Parece error en el original por *Cuba*, como se comprueba mas adelante.
([2]) Acaso *Bohio*, como dice despues.

([1]) It seems to be mistaken for Cuba in the original, as is shown further on. Casas.
([2]) Perhaps Bohio, as he calls it afterwards. Casas.

y así de muchas maneras. Traían azagayas y algunos ovillos de algodon á resgatar, el cual trocaban aquí con algunos marineros por pedazos de vidrio, de tazas quebradas, y por pedazos de escudillas de barro. Algunos dellos traían algunos pedazos de oro colgado al nariz, el cual de buena gana daban por un cascabel destos de pie de gavilano y por cuentecillas de vidrio: mas es tan poco, que no es nada: que es verdad que cualquiera poca cosa que se les dé ellos tambien tenian á gran maravilla nuestra venida, y creian que eramos venidos del cielo. Tomamos agua para los navíos en una laguna que aquí está acerca del *cabo del isleo*, que así la nombré; y en la dicha laguna Martin Alonso Pinzon, capitan de la Pinta, mató otra sierpe tal como la otra de ayer de siete palmos, y fice tomar aquí del linaloe cuanto se falló."

Martes 23 de Octubre.

,, Quisiera hoy partir para la isla de *Cuba*, que creo que debe ser *Cipango* segun las señas que dan esta gente de la grandeza della y riqueza, y no me deterné mas aquí ni([1]) esta isla al rededor para ir á la poblacion, como tenia determinado, para haber lengua con este Rey ó Señor, que es por no me detener mucho, pues veo que aquí no hay mina de oro, y al rodear de estas islas ha menester muchas maneras de viento, y no vienta así como los hombres querrian. Y pues es de andar adonde haya trato grande, digo que no es razon de detener sino ir á camino, y calar mucha tierra fasta topar en tierra muy provechosa, aunque mi entender es questa sea muy provechosa de especería; mas que yo no la cognozeo que llevo la mayor pena del·mundo, que veo mil maneras de árboles que tienen cada uno su manera de fruta, y verde agora como en España en el mes de Mayo y Junio, y mil maneras de yerbas, eso mesmo con flores, y de todo no se cognosció salvo este linaloe de que hoy mandé tambien traer á la nao mucho para llevar á vuestras Altezas. Y no he dado ni doy la vela para *Cuba*, porque no hay viento, salvo calma muerta y llueve mucho; y llovió ayer mucho sin hacer ningun frio, antes el día hace calor, y las noches temperadas como en Mayo en España en el Andalucía."

([1]) Igual vacío en el original.

brought spears and some balls of cotton to barter, which they exchanged here with some sailors for pieces of glass, broken cups, and pieces of earthenware. Some of these few wore pieces of gold in their noses, which they gladly gave away for a small bell such as is attached to the leg of a hawk:([1]) but it is so little that it is nothing: it is true that for any little thing that was given them they marveled greatly at our coming, and thought that we had come down from heaven. We took water for the vessels from a lagoon which is near to the *Cape of the rocky island*, so named by me; and in the said lagoon Martin Alonso Pinzon, captain of the Pinta, killed another serpent like that of yesterday of seven palmos, I caused to be taken on board all the aloes that could be found."

Tuesday October 23d.

" I should like to sail to day for the island of *Cuba*, which from the description about its size and riches given by these people I infer to be Cipango, I will not stop here longer nor([2]) around this island to go to the inhabited portion, as I had determined, in order to have an interview with this king or lord, this is in order not to stop much, because I see that there is no mine of gold here, and to go around these islands requires many different winds, and they do not blow as men would wish. And therefore the most important thing is to go where there is a great trade, I say that it is not right to stop, but to continue on one's course to examine many lands until one reaches some very profitable land, although my idea is that this is very rich in spices; but I grieve exceedingly that I have no knowledge of them, because I see a thousand kinds of trees having each one its own kind of fruit, and green now as in Spain in the month of May and June, and a thousand kinds of herbs, with flowers, of all of which none was known save this aloe of which I have had quantities brought on board the ship for your Highnesses. And I have not sailed nor do I sail for *Cuba*, because there is no wind, but a dead calm and much rain; yesterday it also rained much yet it was not cold, on the contrary it is warm during the day, and the nights are as mild as those of Andalucia in Spain in May.'

([1]) On the plains of Assyria and Babylonia the Arabs use hawks for hunting purposes, to the legs of which are, sometimes, fastened small bells. Layard's *Nineveh and Babylon*, p. 412.

([2]) Blank space in the original. Navarrete.

Miercoles 24 de Octubre.

„Esta noche á media noche levanté las anclas de la isla *Isabela* del *cabo del isleo*, qúes de la parte del Norte á donde yo estaba posado para ir á la isla de *Cuba*, á donde oí desta gente que era muy grande y de gran trato, y había en ella oro y especerías y naos grandes y mercaderes; y me amostró que al Ouesudueste iria á ella, y yo asi lo tengo, porque creo que si es asi como por señas que me hicieron todos los indios de estas islas y aquellos que llevo yo en los navíos, porque por lengua no los entiendo, es la isla de *Cipango* lo que se cuentan cosas maravillosas, y en las esperas que yo ví y en las pinturas de mapamundos es ella en esta comarca, y así navegué fasta el dia al Ouesudueste, y amaneciendo calmó el viento y llovió, y asi casi toda la noche; y estuve así con poco viento fasta que pasaba de medio dia y entonces tornó á ventar muy amoroso, y llevaba todas mis velas de la nao, maestra, y dos bonetas, y trinquete, y cebadera, y mezana, y vela de gavia, y el batel por popa; así anduve al camino fasta que anocheció y entonces me quedaba el *Cabo Verde* de la isla *Fernandina*, el cual es de la parte de Sur á la parte de Oueste, me quedaba al Norueste, y hacía de mí á él siete leguas. Y porque ventaba ya recio y no sabia yo cuanto camino hobiese fasta la dicha isla de *Cuba*, y por no la ir á demandar de noche, porque todas estas islas son muy fondas á no hallar fondo todo en derredor, salvo á tiro de dos lombardas, y esto es todo manchado un pedazo de roquedo y otro de arena, y por esto no se puede seguramente surgir salvo á vista de ojo, y por tanto acordé de amainar las velas todas, salvó el trinquete, y andar con él, y de á un rato crecia mucho el viento y hacía mucho camino de que dudaba, y era muy gran cerrazon, y llovía: mandé amainar el trinquete y no anduvimos esta noche dos leguas &c.‟

Jueves 25 de Octubre.

Navegó despues del sol salido al Oueste Sudueste hasta las nueve horas, andarian cinco leguas: despues mudó el camino al Oueste: andaban ochenta millas por hora hasta la una despues de medio dia, y de allí hasta las tres, y andarian cuarenta y cuatro millas. Entonces

Wednesday October 24th.

"At midnight I weighed anchor from the island of *Isabela* the *cape of the rocky islet*, which is on the northern side where I was lying in order to go to the island of *Cuba*, which I heard from these people was very large, having much trade and that there was in it gold and spices and large ships and merchants; and they told me that I should go to it by the west-southwest, and so I think, because I believe that if it is as all the Indians of these islands and those whom I have on board told me by signs, because I do not understand their language, it is the island of *Cipango* of which marvellous things are related, and on the globes which I have seen and on the maps of the world it is in this region, and thus I sailed until day to the west-southwest, and at dawn the wind calmed and it rained, and so almost all night; and I remained with little wind until after midday and then the wind began to blow very lovely, and I carried all the sails of the ship, the mainsail, two bonnets, the foresail, and spritsail, and the mizzen, and the main-topsail, and the boat astern; thus I followed my course until nightfall and then *Cape Verde* of the island of *Fernandina*, which is towards the south towards the west, remained to the northwest of me, and there was from me to it seven leagues.(¹) The wind was blowing hard and I knew not how far off the island of *Cuba* was, and in order not to approach it at night, because all these islands are so deep that no bottom can be found all around them, save at two lombard shots, and this is all spotted, one piece of rock another of sand, and consequently it is impossible to anchor safely except where you can see, and therefore I determined to lower all the sails, except the foresail, and to sail with that, and suddenly the wind grew very strong and I made much headway of which I was doubtful, and it was very misty, and rained: I had the foresail taken in and we did not go this night two leagues, &c."

Thursday October 25th.

He afterwards sailed from sunrise west-southwest until nine o'clock, making about five leagues: afterward he changed course to the west: they went eight miles an hour until one

(¹) That is, Cape Verde, the southwest end of Fernandina, bore northwest seven leagues distant (22.3 nautical miles).

vieron tierra, y eran siete á ocho islas([1]), en luengo todas de Norte á Sur: distaban de ellas cinco leguas &c.

o'clock p. m., and thence until three o'clock, and they made about forty-four miles. At that time they saw land, and there were seven or eight islands, all extending from north to south: distant from them five leagues, &c.

Viernes 26 de Octubre.

Estuvo de las dichas islas de la parte del Sur, era todo bajo cinco ó seis leguas, surgió por allí. Dijeron los indios que llevaba que habia dellas á *Cuba* andadura de dia y medio con sus almadias, que son navetas de un madero adonde no llevan vela. Estas son las canoas. Partió de allí para *Cuba*, porque por las señas que los indios le daban de la grandeza y del oro y perlas della pensaba que era ella, conviene á saber *Cipango.*

Friday October 26th.

He was on the southern side of said islands, all was shallow for five or six leagues, he anchored there. The Indians he had with him told him that to reach *Cuba* with their canoes from those islands would take them a day and half, these canoes are small vessels of one piece of wood and have no sail. These are the canoes. He sailed thence for *Cuba*, because from the signs which the Indians gave him of the size and of its gold and pearls he thought that was the one, that is to say *Cipango.*

Sabado 27 de Octubre.

Levantó las anclas salido el sol de aquellas islas, que llamó *las islas de Arena* por el poco fondo que tenian de la parte del Sur hasta seis leguas. Anduvo ocho millas por hora hasta la una del dia al Sursudueste, y habrian andado cuarenta millas, y hasta la noche andarian veinte y ocho millas al mesmo camino, y antes de noche vieron tierra. Estuvieron la noche al reparo con mucha lluvia que llovió. Anduvieron el Sabado fasta el poner del sol diez y siete leguas al Sursudueste.

Saturday October 27th.

At sunrise he weighed anchor from those islands, which he called *las islas de Arena* [Sand Islands] on account of the little bottom they had for six leagues to the south. He ran south-southwest at the rate of eight miles an hour until one o'clock in the afternoon, making about forty miles, and up to nightfall they had made about twenty-eight miles on the same course, and before night they saw the land. They were on the lookout during the night with much rain which it rained. They ran on Saturday until sunset seventeen leagues south-southwest.

Domingo 28 de Octubre.

Fue de allí en demanda de la isla de *Cuba* al Sursudueste, á la tierra della mas cercana, y entró en un rio muy hermoso y muy sin peligro de bajas ni otros inconvenientes, y toda la costa que anduvo por allí era muy hondo y muy limpio fasta tierra: tenia la boca del rio doce brazas, y es bien ancha para barloventear; surgió dentro, diz que á tiro de lombarda. Dice el Almirante que nunca tan hermosa cosa vido, lleno de árboles todo cercado el rio, fermosos y verdes y diversos de los nuestros, con flores y con su fruto, cada uno de su manera. Aves muchas y pajaritos que cantaban muy dulcemente: habia gran cantidad de palmas de otra manera que las de Guinea y de las nuestras; de una estatura mediana y los pies sin aquella

Sunday October 28th.

He went thence in search of the island of *Cuba* to the south-southwest, to the land nearest to it [him?], and entered a very beautiful river very free from danger of shoals and other inconveniences, and all the coast that he passed there was very deep and very clear as far as the land: the mouth of the river had twelve fathoms, and is very wide in order to tack in; he anchored within, he said at the distance of a lombard shot. The Admiral says that he never saw such a beautiful thing, the banks of the river being covered with trees, which were beautiful and green and different from ours, with flowers and with their fruit, each one after its kind. Many birds and little birds which sang very sweetly: there was a great quantity of palms different from those of Guinea and from ours; of medium height and the feet without that shirt,([1]) and the leaves very large, with

---

([1]) Deben ser los Cayos orientales y meridionales del *Gran Banco de Bahama*, que despiden placer de sonda al Sur, y donde estuvo fondeado Colon el dia 26 de Octubre, partiendo desde allí para dar vista á *Cuba*; como en efecto la vió entrando el dia 28 en el *puerto de Nipe.*

([1]) He probably found a species of palm that was without the reticulum.

camisa, y las hojas muy grandes, con las cuales cobijan las casas; la tierra muy llana: saltó el Almirante en la barca y fue á tierra, y llegó á dos casas que creyó ser de pescadores y que con temor se huyeron, en una de las cuales halló un perro que nunca ladró, y en ambas casas halló redes de hilo de palma y cordeles, y anzuelo de cuerno, y fisgas de hueso y otros aparejos de pescar, y muchos huegos dentro, y creyó que en cada una casa se juntan muchas personas: mandó que no se tocase en cosa de todo ello, y así se hizo. La yerba era grande como en el Andalucía por Abril y Mayo. Halló verdolagas muchas y bledos. Tornóse á la barca y anduvo por el rio arriba un buen rato, y diz que era gran placer ver aquellas verduras y arboledas, y de las aves que no podia dejallas para se volver. Dice que es aquella isla la mas hermosa que ojos hayan visto, llena de muy buenos puertos y rios hondos, y la mar que parecia que nunca se debia de alzar porque la yerba de la playa llegaba hasta cuasi el agua, la cual no suele llegar donde la mar es brava: hasta entonces no habia experimentado en todas aquellas islas que la mar fuese brava. La isla, dice, ques llena de montañas muy hermosas, aunque no son muy grandes en longura salvo altas, y toda la otra tierra es alta de la manera de Sicilia: llena es de muchas aguas, segun pudo entender de los indios que consigo lleva, que tomó en la isla de *Guanahani*, los cuales le dicen por señas que hay diez rios grandes, y que con sus canoas no la pueden cercar en veinte dias. Cuando iba á tierra con los navíos salieron dos almadías ó canoas, y como vieron que los marineros entraban en la barca y remaban para ir á ver el fondo del rio para saber donde habian de surgir, huyeron las canoas. Decian los indios que en aquella isla habia minas de oro y perlas, y vido el Almirante lugar apto para ellas y almejas, ques señal dellas, y entendia el Almirante que allí venian naos del Gran Can, y graudes, y que de allí á tierra firme habia jornada de diez dias. Llamó el Almirante aquel rio y puerto de *San Salvador*(¹).

which they cover their houses; the land is very level: the Admiral jumped into the ship's boat and went on shore, and came to two houses which ran away in fear, they found in one of them a dog which never barked, and in both houses he found nets of palm thread and cords, and horn fish-hooks, bone harpoons and other fishing-gear, and numerous sets within, and he believed that each house was occupied by many persons: he ordered that nothing in them should be touched, and nothing was. The grass was high as in Andalucia in April and May. He found much purslain and wild amaranth. He returned to the boat and went up the river for a good while, and he said that it was a great pleasure to see that verdure and those groves, and of the birds that he could not leave them in order to return. He says that that island is the most beautiful that eyes ever beheld, full of good ports and deep rivers, and it seemed to him that the sea must never be high there for the grass of the beach almost reached the water, which rarely happens where the sea is rough; until then he had not experienced a rough sea in all those islands. The island, he says, is full of very beautiful mountains, though they are not very long but lofty, and all the land is high like that of Sicily: full of much water, as he could understand from the Indians with him, whom he took from the island of *Guanahani*, who tell him that there are ten large rivers, and that with their canoes they cannot go around it in twenty days. When he went to the land with the vessels two canoes approached, and when they saw that the sailors entered the boat and rowed in order to go to see the bottom of the river in order to know where they were to anchor, the canoes fled. The Indians said that in that island there were mines of gold and pearls, and the Admiral saw place suitable for them and shell-fish, which is a sign of them, and the Admiral understood that ships of the Grand Khan came there, and large ones, and that from there to the main land was a run of ten days. The Admiral called that river and port *San Salvador*.

(¹) Conócese con el nombre de *Puerto ó Bahia de Nipe*, á seis leguas al S. S. E. de la punta de Mulas.

Next to this text in entirety, it is indispensable to every thorough discussion of the first landfall that the student should have before him a correct chart, since an imperfect one is inadequate to the settlement of a problem, the proof of which are certain brief courses. The chart in the appendix was prepared in the office of the U. S. Coast and Geodetic Survey, from the English Admiralty surveys of 1832–1836, and such Spanish charts as were available. The Bahamas, dependent upon the English surveys, are accurate. Some of the harbors, and perhaps part of the coast line of Cuba and Hayti, may be a little in error in longitude.

The five tracks from five different islands tô Cuba are—

1st. Navarrete's from the Grand Turk.
2d. Irving's from Cat.
3d. Captain Becher's from Watling.
4th. Varnhagen's from Mariguana.
5th. G. V. Fox's from Samana, or Atwood Cay.

Although the authorities heretofore mentioned concurred on the first four islands, respectively, it is only those noted here that have laid down a continuous track from the first landfall they claimed for Columbus, to Cuba. With this authentic chart and Las Casas's copy of Columbus's journal, each of these tracks, and the arguments of their supporters, can be tried.

THE TRACK OF NAVARRETE.

Navarrete said, 1st: Columbus sighted the east side of the Grand Turk while steering a course W. by S. ¾ S. and from there he went around by the north, to the west side of the island.

ANSWER. The journal of October 11 says that at sunset—on that day the sun set at $5^h 41^m$ apparent time—Columbus steered west and made the land at 2 a. m. the next day. On the 13th Columbus wrote: "I determined to wait until to-morrow evening, and then to sail for the south-west." On the 14th he wrote that he went *with the boats* "along the island in a north-northeasterly direction, to see the other side," * * * "and afterwards *I returned to the ship*([1]) and set sail."

Navarrete said, 2d: From the west side of the Grand Turk Columbus sailed W. by N. ¼ N. 19 miles to the Caicos Islands which, together, formed the second, to which he gave the name of *Santa Maria de la Concepcion.* (*Navarrete,* p. 26, note I.)

ANSWER. Conceding that Columbus went to the north of west when he said, on the 13th, that he would sail "for the southwest," and admitting the probability that in 1492 the Caicos group ~~was~~ ₍were₎ one island, yet it does not agree with the description of the second island he came to, of which he wrote on the 15th: "And I found that that side which is towards the island of San Salvador runs north [and] south, and is five leagues [15.9 nautical miles] in length, and the other which I followed ran east [and] west, and contains over ten leagues [31.8 nautical miles]. And as from this one I saw another larger one to the west, I clewed up the sails * * * and about sunset I anchored near said cape [the western cape]." The east side of the Caicos is north and south 13 miles, which corresponds with the journal; but the north shore is N. W. by W. ¼ W. 38 miles and then S. W. ¾ W. 38 miles. Or, if the N. E. side of the Caicos group be designated as the east and west side that Columbus followed, it agrees near enough in distance, but varies 2¾ points in direction; and if we assume the journal to be in error in giving "east [and] west," there is still the insurmountable fact that Columbus wrote three times on the 15th, and twice on the 16th, that the third island bore *west* from the second. A vessel anchored at the west cape of the N. E. side of the Caicos group has no land visible. The island of Mariguana is the nearest, and this is N. W. by W. ¼ W. 43 miles distant.

Navarrete said, 3d: From the second island Columbus sailed to the southward and westward to Little Inagua, the third island, which he named Fernandina. (*Navarrete,* p. 28, note I.)

ANSWER. If we take Navarrete's course as it is laid down on the chart, from the west cape of the N. E. side of the Caicos, the course and distance to Little Inagua are S. W. ¼ W. 60 miles. If we measure from the S. W. Caicos to Little Inagua—S. E. side—it is about W. S. W. 25 miles.

On the 15th of October Columbus was at the west cape of his second island and he wrote in regard to the third island, "I saw another larger one to the west * * * and so I departed at about ten o'clock with a S. E. wind, inclining to the south, for the other island, a very large one." * * * And when he came to the third island he said: "All this portion of the island runs N. W. [and] S. E., and it appears that there are on this coast more than 28 leagues [89.1 nautical miles]." On the 16th, after a more careful examination, he wrote: "And this cape to which I have come and all this coast runs N. N. W. and S. S. E. and I saw fully 20 leagues [63.6 nautical miles] of it, but this was not the end."

([1]) *Italics* are by the writer.

This is the description of Ferdinand Island. It cannot be Little Inagua, as Navarrete asserts, because this is only 7½ miles east and west, and the same N. N. E. and S. S. W.

Navarrete said, 4th: From the third island, Little Inagua [Santa Maria], Columbus steered to the southward and westward to the fourth island, Great Inagua, which he named *Isabela*. (*Navarrete*, p. 33, note I.)

ANSWER.. When Columbus left the third island on the 19th of October he wrote: "At dawn I weighed anchor and sent the caravel Pinta to the *east and southeast*, and the caravel Niña *to the S. S. E.*, and I with the ship *went to the S. E.* * * * And then before we had gone three hours we saw an island *to the east*,([1]) to which we directed our course, and all three vessels reached it before midday at its northern extremity, where there is a rocky islet. * * * And the said islet lay from the island of Fernandina, whence I had come, *east* [and] *west*."

Navarrete said, 5th: From the fourth island, Great Inagua [Isabella], Columbus steered N. by E. 11 miles—W. ½ N. 56 miles—W. by N. ¼ N. 61 miles—and S. by W. ¼ W. 61 miles—to Port Nipe, in Cuba.

ANSWER. Such courses and distances cannot be found in Columbus' journal. He left the fourth island on the 24th of October and wrote: "At midnight([2]) I weighed anchor from the island of Isabella, * * * in order to go to the island of Cuba. * * * And they told me that I should go to it by the W. S. W., and so I think. * * * And thus I sailed until day to the W. S. W., and at dawn the wind calmed. * * * And I remained with little wind until after midday and then the wind began to blow very lovely. * * * I followed my course until nightfall, and the Cabo Verde of the island of Fernandina bore N. W. 7 leagues [22.3 nautical miles]."([3])

On the 25th, still steering W. S. W., Columbus discovered "seven or eight islands, all extending from north to south, distant from them five leagues [15.9 nautical miles]." On the 26th the journal reads: "He was on the southern side of said islands, all was shallow for five or six leagues, he anchored there. * * * He sailed thence for Cuba." The journal says, October 27: "At sunrise he weighed anchor from those islands, which he called Sand islands, on account of the little bottom they had for six leagues [19 nautical miles] to the south." Navarrete wrote, in a note, pp. 39–40, that Columbus anchored on the 26th of October on the eastern and southern shoal of the "Grand Bank of Balrama," and left there for Cuba. Although Navarrete's track, on the chart, does not reach this bank, we must admit, from this note, that he intended it. But there is no part of "Columbus Bank" which bears W. S. W. from Great Inagua. Domingo Cay, the most southern part, is W. ½ N. from the most northeastern part of Great Inagua; and the south Ragged island, south of which he anchored, bears W. by N. ¼ N. 155 miles from the N. E. end of Great Inagua, and N. W. by W. ¼ W. 133 miles from the S. W. end. The journal evidently omits some of the distances run from Isabella to the Sand Islands; but on the 24th Columbus gives the bearing and distance of the S. W. Cape of Fernandina, and this "departure" is put on the chart. Afterward he logs 16 leagues W. S. W., then he saw the Sand Islands 5 leagues distant, making a total of 21 leagues, 66.8 nautical miles. The true course and distance from his "departure" to South Ragged are W. S. W. 65 miles. This close agreement may be accidental; but if we omit all distances given, yet the courses found in the journal are irreconcilable with any from Great Inagua to the southeastern Bahama Bank. In respect to Port Nipe, which Navarrete and Captain Becher adopt for Columbus's first anchoring-place in Cuba, see the discussion of Captain Becher's track.

By selecting Turk for the first landfall, an extreme S. E. island of the Bahamas, Navarrete confronts Juan de la Cosa and Antonio Herrera; for on their charts, which will be referred to later, Guanàhani is an island situated *near the middle* of the N. E. side of the Bahama group.

THE TRACK OF VARNHAGEN.

Varnhagen said, 1st: Columbus made the island of Mariguana steering west; he rounded the east end and anchored on the northeast shore. Hence he steered W. ¼ N. 40 miles for Creek Point on Acklin Island; followed the north and south shore for 13 miles, and the east and west shore 29 miles, and so over to the south cape of Long Island.

([1]) *Italics* are by the writer.
([2]) It was obviously the midnight which began this day.
([3]) How could Little Inagua bear N. W. of him 22.3 miles?

ANSWER. Varnhagen, like Navarrete, ignores the assertion of Columbus of October 13: "I determined to wait until to-morrow evening and then to sail for the southwest." He has even omitted this weighty sentence from his *Geschichte des Zeitalters der Entdeckungen.*

Conceding that he steered to the westward from Guanahani, yet Columbus said, on the 15th of October, that the second island he steered for was "over 5 leagues distant, rather 7 [22.3 nautical miles]" but Varnhagen's second island is 40 miles from the first. A difference of 79.4 per cent. in such a short run, *actually gone over*, was not possible with so experienced a navigator. In crossing the Atlantic, a distance of more than 3,000 miles, he overran his log only 11½ per cent. In going from Marignana to Acklin, Columbus went within 5 miles of two islands, each 70 feet high. According to Varnhagen, Columbus does not mention them. It is not characteristic of his journal to omit all notice of the first islands he came to in the New World. He wrote on the 15th of October: "Nevertheless it was my desire not to pass any island, without taking possession of it, as one taken possession of the same may be said of all; and I anchored and remained until to-day."

Columbus did not go along the shore of the second island which runs north and south. He wrote on the 15th of October, "I found that that side which is towards the island of San Salvador runs north [and] south, and is five leagues in length, and *the other which I followed*([1]) ran east [and] west."

Varnhagen said, 2d: Columbus went from the south cape, around Long Island and returned to the south cape.

ANSWER. On the 16th Columbus wrote: "This island is exceedingly large and I have determined to go around it. * * * I set sail with a south wind intending to go around the whole island." * * *

On the 17th he wrote: "The wind then ceased, and then sprang up from the W. N. W., which was contrary to our course, and so I turned around and sailed all the past night. * * * And we [are] at the S. E. cape of the island where I hope to anchor until it gets clear." In addition to these decisive words, there is the fact, shown by the chart, that between Exuma and Long Island the water is too shoal for such vessels as Columbus used. This will be spoken of again in discussing Irving's track.

Varnhagen said, 3d: Columbus sailed from the south cape of Long Island to the N. W. end of Crooked Island, then across the "Columbus bank" to Port Gibara, in Cuba.

ANSWER. This part of Varnhagen's track comes near to Captain Becher's and the writer's, and therefore need not be considered here except in regard to the harbor of Gibara. In the journal of October 28th we read: "He went thence in search of the island of Cuba, * * * and entered a very beautiful river * * * the mouth of the river had *twelve fathoms.*"([2]) The port of Gibara is a small basin, exposed to northerly winds, and has only *three fathoms* at the entrance.

WASHINGTON IRVING'S TRACK.

The track of Washington Irving is laid down from his description of the "Route of Columbus in his first voyage." (*Irving's Columbus*, revised edition, vol. iii, appendix, pp. 366–380.)

Irving wrote, 1st: "From Guanahani Columbus saw so many islands that he was at a loss which next to visit. * * * He determined to go to the largest in sight. * * * The island thus selected, it is presumed, was the present island of Conception; and that the others were that singular belt of small islands known as La Cardena (or the chain) stretching past the island of San Salvador in a S. E. and N. W. direction; the nearest of the group being nearer than Concepcion, while the rest are more distant. * * * We know that in all this neighborhood the current sets strongly to the W. N. W.; and since Columbus had the current against him he must have been sailing in an opposite direction, or to the E. S. E." Hence it is rendered certain that Columbus did not sail westward in going from San Salvador to Conception; for from the opposition of the wind, as there could be no other cause, he could not sail toward that quarter. * * * Conception situated E. S. E. from San Salvador, and at a corresponding distance of 5 leagues [15.9 nautical miles]."

([1]) *Italics* are by the writer.
([2]) E. F. Qualtrough, Master U. S. Navy. *Sailors' Handy Book*, p. 192, makes the old Spanish braza equal 5.432 English feet. *Italics* are by the writer.

App. 18——5

ANSWER. Columbus wrote, on the 14th of October: "I returned to the ship and set sail and saw so many islands that I could not decide to which one I should go first." Mr. Gibbs made personal observation from the southeast point of Cat island and wrote: "No land can be seen from the highest hills, nor from the mast-head of a vessel lying at Winding Bay or Columbus Point, where he is said to have landed.[1]

The island of Conception is 2¾ miles long, 1½ broad, and 90 feet high. Near by, on the east side, is Booby Cay, one-third of a mile across and 130 feet high. The reef surrounding both is 8 by 5 miles. It is possible that in 1492 an island might have been there of these dimensions.

On the 15th of October Columbus described the second island thus: "I found that that side which is toward the island of San Salvador runs north [and] south, and is five leagues [15.9 nautical miles] in length, and the other which I followed ran east [and] west, and contains over ten leagues"—31.8 nautical miles. La Cardena (the chain of islands stretching away to the northward and westward from Great Exuma) is, in the nighest part, 36 miles from Cat island, 48 from Columbus Point, and 50 from Conception, and certainly invisible from each.

The currents in this neighborhood are spoken of by Capt. E. Barnet in the *West India Pilot*, 3d edition, 1876, p. 431, thus: "In the neighborhood of Conception Island it is said generally to run strong to the N. W. Some observations tend to show that after northers or on the increase of the moon, as it approaches to change, there is a similar set to the southward. There is, however, no certainty in the case, and consequently more than ordinary attention is required when navigating among the West India islands."

There is no foundation that Columbus had "the current against him," except his remark of the 13th of October, "the tide detained me." On the eve of leaving Guanahani he wrote, "I determined to wait until tomorrow evening, and then to sail for the southwest." There is no mention in the journal of "the opposition of the wind." Columbus does not give its direction until the 15th, when he was at the second island, then he records it as being S. E. Conception lies S. S. E. ¼ E., 19 miles from the southeast point of Cat.

Irving wrote, 2d: "Leaving Conception on the 16th of October Columbus steered for a very large island seen to the westward nine leagues [28.6 nautical miles] off, and which extended itself 28 leagues [89 nautical miles] in a southeast and northwest direction. * * * He named it Fernandina. At noon he made sail again, with a view to run round it and reach another island called Samoet; but the wind being at S. E. by S. the course he wished to steer, the natives signified that it would be easier to sail around the island by running to the N. W. with a fair wind. He therefore bore up to the N. W., and having run two leagues [6.4 nautical miles] found a marvelous port with a narrow entrance. * * * Sailing out of this harbor by the opposite entrance at the northwest, he discovered that part of the island which runs east and west. The natives signified to him that this island was smaller than Samoet, and that it would be better to return towards the latter. It had now become calm, but shortly after there sprung up a breeze from the W. N. W., which was ahead for the course they had been steering; so they bore up and stood to the E. S. E. in order to get an offing; for the weather threatened a storm, which however dissipated itself in rain. The next day, being the 18th of October, they anchored opposite the extremity of Fernandina. The whole of this description answers most accurately to the island of Exuma. * * * The identity of the island here described with Exuma is irresistibly forced upon the mind."

ANSWER. In calling Exuma Fernandina, and anchoring Columbus "opposite the extremity," it is evident that Irving included in this name Little Exuma, which lies to the southward and eastward of Great Exuma, and Hog Cay lying farther east. These might have formed one island in 1492, for the narrow channel between Great and Little Exuma is now almost fordable at low water. On this chart Great Exuma and Hog Cay only are noted. The land between is Little Exuma.

From Conception Irving takes Columbus to a position, whence, by steering at least 6.4 miles N. W., he came to, entered, and passed through "a marvellous port" (Great Exuma harbor). It is obvious that the opposite of northwest, measured 6.4 miles from the southeast entrance of this harbor, would put a ship on shore; therefore the track on this chart is laid down close to the land, without regard to the course it makes.

---

[1] Proceedings of the New York Historical Society, 1846. Appendix.

From Conception to the turning-point of Irving, 6.4 miles to the eastward of Great Exuma harbor, the course and distance are S. W. ½ S., 35 miles. While on his way from the second island to the third—Conception to Fernandina—October 15th, Columbus wrote: "And from this island of Santa Maria to the other one there are 9 leagues [28.6 nautical miles] east [and] west." On the 16th, after arriving at Fernandina, he wrote: "This island lies at a distance from that of Santa Maria 8 leagues [25.5 nautical miles] almost east [and] west."

He could not have entered and sailed out of this marvellous port by the opposite entrance, because on the 17th of October he said: "I found a very marvellous port. * * * Within it there is ample room for 100 ships if it had sufficient depth of water and was clear, and also had a deep entrance. I thought it worth while to examine and sound it, and so I anchored outside of it, and went in with all the boats of the ships and saw there was not bottom." Neither could he have discovered that part of Exuma which runs east and west, because no part of it does. Nor could he have anchored opposite the extremity of Fernandina, because there is not sufficient depth of water.

Irving wrote, 3d: "On the 19th of October the ships left Fernandina steering S. E., with the wind at north. Sailing three hours on this course they discovered Samoet to the east, and steered for it, arriving at its north point before noon. Here they found a little island surrounded by rocks, with another reef of rocks lying between it and Samoet. To Samoet Columbus gave the name of Isabella, and to the point of it opposite the little island, that of Cabo del Isleo; the cape of the S. W. point of Samoet Columbus called Cabo de Laguna, and off this last his ships were brought to anchor. The island lay in the direction from Fernandina to Isabella, east and west. The coast from the small island lay westerly 12 leagues [38.2 nautical miles] to a cape which Columbus called Formosa, from its beauty; this he believed to be an island apart from Samoet or Isabella, with another between them. Leaving Cabo Laguna, where he remained until the 20th of October, Columbus steered to the N. E. toward Cabo del Isleo, but meeting with shoals inside the small island, he did not come to anchor until the day following. * * * The island of Isabella, or Samoet, agrees so accurately in its description with Isla Larga [Long Island], which lies east of Exuma, that it is only necessary to read it with the chart unfolded to become convinced of its identity."

ANSWER. This is the description of that part of the Bahamas which the *West India Pilot*, vol. ii, p. 444, describes thus: "The west side of Long Island is only navigable for boats and very small coasters, who manage to pick their way across to the Jumento cays." The blank space on this chart from Exuma to Long Island was purposely left so by the English surveyors, because it is unnavigable. There is no ground for believing that the water was deeper in 1492, for the wasting of these islands and cays tends to the opposite result.

Irving makes Columbus leave Exuma [Fernandina] in search of Samoet, which, he says, is Long Island. Now when Columbus was at Conception he had Long Island plainly in sight, for it is only 14 miles from there. In fact, to go from Conception to Exuma, an island he could not see, he had to bend his course to the northward and westward to avoid an island that was visible at his start and for which he was searching.

Irving wrote, 4th: "Having resolved to visit the island which the natives called Cuba, and described as bearing W. S. W. from Isabella, Columbus left Cabo del Isleo at midnight, the commencement of the 24th of October, and shaped his course accordingly to the W. S. W. * * * and in the evening Cape Verd, S. W. point of Fernandina [Exuma], bore N. W. distant 7 leagues [22.3 nautical miles]. * * * At 3 p. m. of the 25th land was discovered, consisting of 7 or 8 keys, lying north and south, and distant 5 leagues [15.9 nautical miles] from the ship. Here he anchored the next day, south of these islands, which he called Islas de Arena. * * * This sum of 30 leagues [95.5 nautical miles] is about three less than the distance from the S. W. point of Fernandina or Exuma, whence Columbus took his departure, to the group of the Mucarras, which lie east of Cayo Lobo on the grand bank of Bahama, and which correspond to the description of Columbus. * * * The course from Exuma to the Mucarras is about S. W. by W. * * * At sunrise Columbus set sail from the isles Arenas or Mucarras for an island called Cuba, steering S. S. W. At dark, having made 17 leagues [54.1 nautical miles] on that course, he saw the land and hove his ship to until morning. On the 28th he made sail again at S. S. W. and entered a beautiful river with a fine harbor, which he named San Salvador. * * * This port of San Salvador we take to be the one now known as Caravelas Grandes."

ANSWER. Columbus wrote on the 24th of October: "At midnight I weighed anchor from the island of Isabela the cape of the rocky islet, which is on the northern side where I was lying in order to go to the island of Cuba." On the 19th, when he had anchored at this rocky islet, he wrote: "The coast afterwards ran from the rocky islet to the westward, and there was in it twelve leagues as far as a cape, which I called Cape Beautiful, which is in the west." These extracts point out that the rocky islet from which Columbus sailed for Cuba had land stretching from it to the westward, which terminated in a beautiful cape. Muñoz, Irving, and also M. le Baron de Montlezun, make this position to be the northwest end of Long Island.(¹) But thence no land runs to the westward, nor could Columbus's vessels go to Cuba from there, because of shallow water.

The bearing and distance which Columbus gives on the 24th of October, "S. W. cape of Fernandina N. W. 7 leagues [22.3 nautical miles]" Irving reckons from the southeast end of Exuma. This is marked on the chart "departure." The course to it from the rocky islet—northwest end of Long Island—is S. by E. When Columbus left the cape of the rocky islet, on the 24th of October, he wrote: "And thus I sailed until day to the W. S. W." A course from the northwest end of Long Island to Irving's "departure" passes over the shallow water spoken of, and goes through the solid land which stretches from Long Island.

From this departure, Irving makes Columbus go straight to the Mucarras Reef. A glance at the chart shows the impossibility of such a course. It runs through cays, among "rocky heads," and over that very shoal part of the Bahama bank upon which the experienced seaman hesitates to venture even with a good pilot and a correct chart.

Columbus's journal does not speak of any shoal water from the cape of the rocky islet to the "islas de Arena." When he arrived there it reads: "He was on the southern side of said islands, all was shallow for five or six leagues [15.8 to 19.1 nautical miles], he anchored there." According to the chart, there is no shallow water south of the Mucarras; the deep water of the old Bahama channel runs close to it.

From Mucarras to the port of Caravelas Grandes it is S. S. W. ⅓, W. only 28 miles. Irving admits that Columbus ran on the 27th 17 leagues—54.1 nautical miles—and, on the 28th, more on the same course. But fifty-four miles from the Mucarras, in a south-southwest direction, is 26 miles into the island of Cuba. The port of Caravelas Grandes has 6 feet of water at the entrance and the tide rises 3½ feet. The journal of October 28th reads: "The mouth of the river had twelve fathoms." Even if this is a clerical error it is certain that the flag-ship of Columbus could not enter so shallow a port. (See Appendix E.)

All that Muñoz wrote in regard to the identity of Watling and Guanahani and the track of Columbus in the Bahamas is this, in volume 1—the only one published, owing to his death—pp. 85-86: "In my opinion, Guanahani is Watlin. He landed on the S. W. point. He took the boats and reconnoitered by way of the N. N. E. the western coast, and having doubled the northern point, he turned around by the eastern coast, which is the largest side and is estimated at having more than 15 leagues(²) [47.7 nautical miles]."

Page 87 : "Having stayed three days at San Salvador, he sailed to a smaller island which he had descried, at the distance of 7 leagues [22.3 nautical miles]; without stopping there, he steered for another and larger one, which seemed to lie at a distance of about 10 leagues [31.8 nautical miles] to the west. Here he cast anchor and took possession of the land, calling it Santa Maria de la Concepcion. * * * Hence continuing 8 leagues [25.4 nautical miles] in a westerly direction, he came upon an island which was considerably larger, level, pleasant, and having a beautiful beach. I think it is the island which is called Gato [Cat], which he called Fernandina."

Page 88 : "Having turned the prows to the S. E., the fleet passed an island superior to those which they had seen, both in extent and pleasant appearance; it rose higher above the surface of the sea; the soil was not so uniform as in the others, but varied, with some hills; it abounded in water, many lagoons, and most beautiful meadows and groves. He took possession

(¹) According to Irving's text, ante, 3d, Columbus's track on this chart, on the west side of Long Island, should be extended to the "north point."

(²) To row around Watling island, the distance is 39 nautical miles; around Cat, it is 100.

and changed its former name Samoeto to Isabéla. It is probably that which is now called Long Island."

Page 90: "He steered to the south, in quest of the large land which was mentioned by all the people of the Lucayos islands under the name of Cuba. They referred to it with expressions and gestures which seemed to our men to signify abundance of gold and pearls, great nations, powerful kings, many ships, seamen, and merchants. Having compared these circumstances with the place where the map of Toscanelli represented the extreme portion of India and its adjacent islands, Columbus and the Pinzons suspected that this Cuba was the famous Cipango. They sighted it on the 27th of October, at nightfall, on the northern coast. At dawn on the following day they saw, in taking their first view, a most beautiful country, very remarkable; beautiful rising grounds and mountains, wide-stretching meadow lands, and rivers of considerable volume. In one of these the fleet anchored," &c.

Muñoz, probably, had no authentic chart when he wrote the above. The east side of Watling is only twelve miles long. If Columbus went from Watling *to* a smaller island, without stopping at the latter, it was either Conception or Rum Cay. From neither could he have sailed to the west 31.8 miles and then taken possession of any land except—with some allowance—the northwest part of Long Island. From here he could not continue in a *westerly* direction 25.4 miles and arrive at Cat, because this lies about *north by west* from that. After leaving Cat, he turns his prows to the southeast, returns, and takes possession of the island he left a few days before. As Muñoz means that Columbus went to Cuba, steering south from the northwest end of Long Island, see the discussion of Irving's track (*ante*, p. 36).

CAPTAIN BECHER'S TRACK.

Captain A. B. Becher, Royal Navy, published in London, in 1856, an octavo of 376 pages, called the *Landfall of Columbus on his first voyage to America*. In the preface he wrote: "The work has cost several years of close application at frequent intervals of rest from the duties of the Hydrographical Office of the Admiralty." In 1856 the accurate Admiralty charts used in this discussion had been published. The office in which Captain Becher served possessed more knowledge about the Bahamas than is known elsewhere, and his position gave him exceptional advantages in seeking information. With such facts it might be expected that his conclusions should be generally accepted.

Captain Becher first makes Columbus approach Watling steering S. W., and he anchors him on the northeast side, about four miles east-southeast of the northeast end, in a position from which his boats must have rowed northwest "to see the other side." He also takes the squadron around Watling by the north.

ANSWER. The journal of October 11 reads: "He sailed to the west-southwest. * * * After sunset he sailed on his first course to the west; they went about 12 miles an hour [9.6 nautical miles], and two hours after midnight they had run about 90 miles, that is, 22½ leagues [71.6 nautical miles]. * * * Two hours after midnight the land appeared about two leagues off [6.4 nautical miles]." Columbus wrote on the 14th: "At dawn I ordered the boat of the ship and the boats of the caravels to be got ready, and went along the island, in a north-northeasterly direction, to see the other side, which was on the other side of the east, and also to see the villages." After he had examined the island in the boats on the 14th, he wrote: "And afterward I returned to the ship and set sail."

Captain Becher writes, 2d Appendix, page 345, note: "Rum Cay is the name of the small island first steered for by Columbus after leaving Guanahani, and on which he not only did not consider it worth while to land, but even not to bestow a name."

Pages 111, 112: "The distance of Rum Cay corresponds with that given by Columbus, but he was mistaken in respect of its size, and no doubt baffled and deceived from the effects of the current. Yet no sooner does he gain it than, attracted by another large island to the westward, without waiting to land on this, 'the first island steered for,' he continues his course toward that, making all the sail he can, so as to reach it before night."

Page 116: "But with respect to the size of Rum Cay, it is evidently erroneously stated in the journal; perhaps from accident, arising from the blotted and rotten condition of the papers. But Columbus, seeing it was an unimportant island, and that a much larger one was before him, hastens off to it, and could not, therefore, say anything for certain about Rum Cay. If he really meant the length of its side next to Guanahani and that lying east and west to be as he gives them, they are greatly in error. But this requires confirmation; and it might be asked how he could have determined the former? All this must have been mere guesswork, for he could not get to the southward, being prevented by the current.

ANSWER. Rum Cay is only 4½ miles north and south, and 9½ east and west. If the reef around it is included, it would measure 8 miles north and south and 12½ east and west. Columbus wrote of the second island, on the 15th of October: "And I found that that side, which is toward the island of San Salvador, runs north [and] south, and is five leagues [15.9 nautical miles] in length, and the other which I followed ran east [and] west, and contains over ten leagues [31.8 nautical miles]. And as from this island I saw another larger one to the west, I clewed up the sails for I had gone all that day until night, because I could not yet have gone to the western cape, to which I gave the name of the island of Santa Maria de la Concepcion, and about sunset I anchored near said cape in order to learn whether there was gold there."

Columbus said, in his letter to Luis de Santangel, Navarrete, p. 167: "To the first island that I found I gave the name of San Salvador. * * * To the second island I gave the name of Santa Maria de Concepcion; the third I called Fernandina; the fourth, Isabela; the fifth, Juana," &c. These extracts from Columbus and Captain Becher are contradictory. Captain Becher's strain at an agreement is at the expense of Columbus, and his surmises show the insurmountable obstacle of selecting Rum Cay for the second island. The substance of Columbus's journal is this: he sailed over 31⅙ miles along a shore of the second island, which ran east and west; then he saw a larger island to the west; he took in sail; he named the second island and he anchored at the west cape of it, and the next day he went on shore there.

Captain Becher, Appendix, p. 345, note xxix, translates "Cargue las velas"—*crowds all sail;* the true meaning is, *I clewed up the sails.* On p. 118 Captain Becher again recognizes the perplexity of his situation, for after saying that Columbus did nôt bestow a name on the second island he writes: "But why should 'Rum Cay' be thus left nameless?" And thereupon he proposes this tampering with the names given by Columbus (p. 118). "The long appellation of Santa Maria de la Concepcion is, therefore, divided between Rum Cay and Long Island; the name Concepcion being assigned to the former, and to the latter, Long Island, Santa Maria, or St. Mary." On page 376 he recalls this extraordinary division, and suggests that the whole of Long Island should be called Concepcion, and the northwest cape, Santa Maria. Captain Becher asks how Columbus could have determined the length of the side of the island next to Guanahani, as the current prevented his going to the southward, and he remarks that it must have been mere "guesswork." On the 15th of October Columbus speaks of being late in arriving at the second island, because "the tide detained me." He says nothing about the "current" preventing his course to the south. Of the two sides of the island he saw, he chose to follow the one running east and west, without giving any reason therefor. His estimate of the length of the side he did not follow *was* "guesswork." Navigators of the present day necessarily enter upon their log-books a great deal of guesswork, especially in regard to new lands, and they will continue to do so.

Captain Becher writes, 3d (p. 118): "Columbus passed along the northern shore of Rum Cay without landing on it, and continued to the west under all the sail he could set for Cape Santa Maria de la Concepcion." * * *

Pages 120, 121. "Columbus is now approaching that portion of his discoveries where he has been least understood, and yet where his journal is by no means deficient in clearness and perspicuity; still his actual proceedings, and their localities, seemed to have escaped the penetration of all who have attempted to connect them. But here in fact, he was deceived himself, believing that he was alluding to one island when he was really speaking of two, thereby baffling investigation without intending to do so, and puzzling effectually the ingenuity of all geographers. Among other reasons, such as the state of the wind, &c., for not delaying his stay at Cape Santa Maria, is the appearance of another large island in the west. He, therefore, makes sail for it, about 10 a.m., with a S. E. wind, borrowing, as seamen term it (that is edging) toward the south, that he might look down along the western shore of the island, as he would open it when rounding Cape Santa Maria."

Pages 121–122: "The wind, however, does not allow of his making much progress to the south. It falls in light airs, comes more from the southward against him, so that his course becomes more westerly, and he approaches the southern portion of the Exuma Islands." * * *

Page 122. "And before he arrives at it, while it is yet before him, he gives it the name of Fernandina, not having given any name even to that of Cape Santa Maria."

Page 126: "The 17th of October, the Admiral is at anchor off the island called Great Exuma. * * * The course which Columbus pursued from Guanahani to Concepcion (considered here to be Rum Cay, although not named by the Admiral), and from thence to Cape Santa Maria de Concepcion (believed here also to be the north extreme of Long Island), and from this to Exuma, which is agreed on as being Fernandina, appears on the accompanying chart."

ANSWER. On the 15th of October Columbus was at the western cape of an island which he called Santa Maria de la Concepcion, considered by Captain Becher to be the north end of Long Island. Then, and on that date, Columbus wrote: "From this island I saw another larger one to the west. * * * And soon after I set sail for the other large island that appeared at the west. * * * And so I left, at about ten o'clock, with a southeast wind inclining to the south for the other island. * * * And from this island of Santa Maria to the other one there are nine leagues [28.6 nautical miles] east and west."

On the 16th he wrote: "About noon I left the *islands of Santa Maria de la Concepcion* for the *island of Fernandina*, which appears to be very large to the west, and I sailed all that day with calm weather." On the same date, having arrived at Fernandina, he writes: "This island lies at a distance from that of Santa Maria of eight leagues [25.5 nautical miles] almost east [and] west."

Assuming that the masthead lookout of the flag-ship was 60 feet above the sea, the range of visibility for the horizon is 8.85 nautical miles. There is no part of Great Exuma over 100 feet high, the range of visibility of which is 11.42 nautical miles, total 20.27 miles.([1]) The land which bears west from the north end of Long Island is the northwest end of Exuma, distant 38 miles, and it is, of course, invisible. The entrance of Exuma harbor, to which Captain Becher takes Columbus, pp. 132–133, is S. W. by W. 24 miles from Cape Santa Maria, and the island about 2 miles farther. At the distance of 26 miles it is below the horizon, but sometimes, especially at nightfall, clouds form which make a strong resemblance to land.

Had Columbus meant to go from Santa Maria to the southward and westward, he might believe that he saw land there. But he did not sail in that direction; he did not "edge" to the south; he did not "look along the western shore"; he reiterates that he saw land *to the west*, and he went there. Captain Becher easily satisfies himself in respect to the views he holds in contradiction to Columbus, by saying that he "deceived himself"; was "baffling investigation," and "puzzling effectually the ingenuity of all geographers."

Captain Becher writes 4th, pages 132–133, that Columbus sailed from Exuma harbor, "where he had now obtained water, * * * about noon of Wednesday, the 17th of October," and "the ships all make sail on a north-northwest course."

Pages 134–135: "When they were about two leagues from the cape, or extreme of the island, he observes what he supposes to be the mouth of a river, and is induced to anchor his ships off it. * * * Instead of a river they find what would be a harbor large enough to contain all the ships of Christendom (a favorite expression of Columbus), if it were not deficient in depth, a no less essential quality, indeed, than superficial extent for the formation of a harbor. It is described as having two entrances formed by an island, yet very narrow and with little water in them. The harbor, from this description, seems to correspond with a part of the shore of the island about ten miles to the N. W. of the former harbor (Exuma), but is really nothing more than the low shelving shore of the island covered to the depth of a few feet by the sea."

Page 137: "After staying a couple of hours at this anchorage and obtaining water, the boats return to their ships, and Columbus continues his north-northwest course along the island. The

([1]) From the table of distances at which objects can be seen at sea in nautical miles—used by the U. S. Light House Board.

wind meanwhile seems to have died away, and the ships no sooner arrive off the extreme of the island than they are becalmed; not, however, very long, for soon afterwards it springs up again from the west-northwest, which, as Columbus observes in his journal, was fair for where they had come from, * * * on which he claps his helm up and stands away to the eastward."

ANSWER. When Columbus left Santa Maria for Fernandina, on the 16th of October, he wrote: "I could not arrive in time to see the bottom in order to get a clear anchorage, a thing requiring the greatest care in order not to lose the anchors; in consequence I waited until daylight when I anchored near a village. * * * And this cape to which I have come, and all this coast runs northwest and southeast." October 17th he wrote: "At midday I left the village where I had anchored and taken in water, in order to sail around this island of Fernandina. * * * I sailed to the north-northwest, and when I was near the end of the island, two leagues off [6.4 nautical miles], I found a very marvellous port with an entrance, although it may be said that there are two entrances, because it has a rocky islet in the middle, and both are very narrow, but within it there is ample room for one hundred ships if it had sufficient depth of water and was clear, and also had a deep entrance: I thought it worth while to examine and sound it, and so I anchored outside of it, and went in with all the boats of the ships, and saw that there was not bottom. And because I thought when I saw it that it was the mouth of some river I had the casks sent on shore for water. * * * After getting in water I returned to the ship, and set sail, and sailed to the northwest until I discovered all that part of the island as far as the coast which runs east [and] west."

Captain Becher anchors Columbus off Exuma harbor, where his vessels take in some water. He does not say which entrance, but from his track it appears to be the southeast one. The series of connected harbors formed by Elizabeth and Stocking islands and the adjacent cays, on the northeast side of Exuma, are the best in the Bahamas. They are from $\frac{1}{4}$ to $\frac{1}{2}$ a mile wide, and have two entrances, $7\frac{1}{2}$ miles apart. The southeast one has 18 feet at low water and the northwest one 21 feet. The tide rises $2\frac{1}{2}$ feet. Beginning at the southeast is Elizabeth harbor, with from 21 to 23 feet; Stocking with 16; Conch 15 to 24, and at the northwest Exuma with 31. These harbors are generally known by the name of "Exuma," and they will be so called in this paper. Captain Becher had the Admiralty plans, and the description of each, in his office, and therefore knew that Exuma could not be the "marvellous port" which Columbus examined and found too shoal. Hitherto Columbus had been casting anchor on the reefs surrounding the islands, and his anxiety therefrom found expression in his journal of the 15th and 16th of October. Can anyone be made to comprehend, that when he had "voyaged the unreal, vast, unbounded deep," and arrived off a series of sheltered harbors, he did not go in and anchor; did not even mention them in his journal; but sailed away from these, which had sufficient depth, to the northwest 10 miles, where he found a "marvellous port which had ample room for 100 ships"— not "all the ships of Christendom," as Captain Becher translates it—but was too shallow; and that this "marvellous port" described so minutely by Columbus—because a harbor deep enough for his vessels to enter was the necessity of his situation—Captain Becher dismisses by saying that it corresponds "with a part of the shore about ten miles to the northwest of the former harbor [Exuma], but is really nothing more than the low shelving shore of the island covered to the depth of a few feet by the sea."

If Columbus's track had been along the shore of Exuma, as laid down by Captain Becher, he could not have found a port with insufficient water; he would have discovered those excellent harbors ample for his needs, which may be seen on the British Admiralty charts—"Special plans of the Bahama Bank" and "Harbors of Great Exuma, number 390"—and he would certainly have anchored therein.

Captain Becher writes, 5th, pp. 137-140: "But trouble is at hand. Columbus says, he had experienced rain every day more or less since he had been among the islands. He was now to endure the discomforts of a heavy gale, the first he had met with in the New World. * * * The breeze before which the Admiral bore up soon freshens, and he runs before it to the E. S. E., making good this course, steering sometimes east and sometimes southeast, the first part of it to keep off the land, the courses being altered as necessary. The first part of these courses would take him from his position where he bore up towards and well clear of Cape Santa Maria; and with the southeast course his ships would bound along before the gale at no great distance from the outer shore of Long Island (the wind drawing northerly as he proceeded), while he was under the impression, from the direction in which the southeast part of Exuma Island lies, which he had seen, that the southern part of Long Island was that same Fernandina he had left on the previous day. The deception would be completed in the mind of Columbus, first, by the direction in which Exuma lies, being the same as the southern part of Long Island; and, next, by losing sight of this island when obscured at intervals of the storm and by the darkness of the night, in which he was either lying by or running to the southward; for the journal tells us that, as the weather permitted, the ships continued running before the wind towards the southeast point of the island, which having reached they passed round it sufficiently to find shelter, and soon found a smooth anchorage. This mistake of the Admiral in believing that he was now at anchor off the southeast end of Exuma, which he had named Fernandina, when he was really off Long Island, is thus quite admissible. He had undergone the ordeal of a gale accompanied by heavy rain, and in the obscurity of this and the darkness of night he must frequently have lost sight of the land, anxious as he was to keep it on board, and at the same time fearful of getting too near it. His conclusion was formed on fair grounds, but under circumstances which rendered him very liable to be deceived as he was; for he was now at anchor snugly sheltered from the sea with his fleet under the southeast end of Long Island, or, as he supposed, Fernandina, to which island the name Santa Maria has been assigned, as given by himself to the northwest cape of it, that of Fernandina being left for Exuma, on which island it was undoubtedly bestowed by the Admiral."

ANSWER. The substance of these extracts is, that from the northwest end of Great Exuma Columbus made good an E. S. E. course to clear Cape Santa Maria, before a wind which freshened into a gale; that during the night of October 17-18 there *was* a heavy gale accompanied by rain; that the ships rounded the cape and "bound along before the gale at no great distance from the outer shore of Long Island;" that sometimes the land was obscured by the storm and the darkness of the night; and that finally he arrived safe at the southeast end of the island, but, for reasons given, he believed he was at anchor at the southeast end of Exuma.

Columbus, under date of October 17, but obviously written on the 18th, said: "And so I turned around and sailed all the past night to the east-southeast, and sometimes wholly east and sometimes to the southeast; this I did in order to keep off the land for the atmosphere was very misty and the weather threatening: it [the wind] *was light* and did not permit me to reach the land in order to anchor. So that this night it rained very hard after midnight until almost day, and is still cloudy in order to rain; and we [are] at the southeast cape of the island where I hope to anchor until it gets clear in order to see the other islands where I have to go." On the 18th, continuing these remarks, he wrote, "After it cleared up I followed the wind, and went around the island as much as I could, and I anchored when it was no longer possible to sail."

From the northwest end of Great Exuma to the northwest end of Long Island it is east 38 miles, hence about S. E. by S. ¼ S. 57 to the southeast cape and 5 more to the south end; total 100 miles. The sun rose October 17 at 6ʰ 20ᵐ and set at 5ʰ 40ᵐ apparent time; twilight lasted 1ʰ 19ᵐ, so that the darkness of that night was very little more than 10 hours. It is essential to Captain Becher's case that the vessels of Columbus shall be gotten to the south cape of Long Island, but he cannot take them the shortest way, between Long Island and Exuma, as Irving did, because the surveys made since he examined the subject show this to be impossible. Therefore he seeks to extricate himself from the dilemma by inventing a storm for the night of October 17-18.

There is not a word in the journal to authorize Captain Becher's assertion in regard to the weather of this night. Kettell's translation, p. 51, is this: "The weather being cloudy and thick it rained violently from midnight till near day, and the sky still remains cloudy." Major, journal of the Royal Geographical Society, volume xli, p. 200: "There was little wind and it did not allow me to put in to anchor. So it rained very heavily from midnight till near daybreak." Irving, revised edition, Life of Columbus, volume iii, appendix: "For the weather threatened a storm, which, however, dissipated itself in rain." Columbus says of the wind, *el era poco,* "it was light." All his other words, and his actions, show the truth of this. He was among islands which he had observed were surrounded by reefs, and at "two lombard shots" no bottom; he had felt the influence of the tides, and now, at night, with thick weather, *but light winds,* his anxiety "to reach the land in order

App. 18——6

to anchor," and thus maintain his position rather than drift, was what might be expected of a prudent and skilful seaman.

If Columbus had "made good" a course E. S. E. from the northwest end of Exuma he would have run on shore about 12 miles south of the northwest end of Long Island. Little Exuma, considered by Captain Becher to be also Exuma—and so allowed in this discussion—lies west-northwest and east-southeast, while the south part of Long Island is north-northwest and south-southeast.

In Captain Becher's track from Rum Cay to Exuma he anchors Columbus, on the evening of October 15, at the northwest end of Long Island. The next morning the Admiral went on shore, but returned and sailed on or before noon. During this short visit he had no opportunity to inspect the shore line of the island, neither could he possibly know the direction of that part which lay beyond the range of visibility from his masthead, a distance only of 8.85 miles (*ante*, p. 39).

Although at this time Columbus had been but four days among the Bahamas, he noted in his journal the dangers of the navigation and the care which he took to shun them.

Captain Becher ought to have reached the conviction that such a seaman and navigator as Columbus would not start his squadron from the northwest end of Great Exuma and steer between Rum Cay and Conception on the one side, and Long Island on the other, and then coast the whole length of the latter 60 miles, 50 *of which were unknown to him, in a dark night, during a gale of wind, in thick rainy weather, and so near the coral reefs circling the island that he saw the latter in the intervals of the storm.*

This night had about ten hours of darkness (*ante*, p. 41), and the distance run along Captain Becher's track is 100 nautical miles, equal to 10 nautical, or ~~about~~ 12 Italian miles, every hour, an unprecedented speed. This might be conceded, but in no circumstances such as Captain Becher mentions should a seaman attempt to steer for and then haul around Long Island, except there was a light on the northwest end. Neither would a seaman *coast the shore of unknown land during darkness and storm*, no matter what the urgency might be. The fruit of blundering seamanship like this can be found in the record of shipwrecks along the Bahama reefs.[1]

In navigating among such islands a commander is sometimes compelled to take the present risk in order to escape an impending disaster. But Captain Becher laid no such stress upon Columbus. He "bounds him along" the reef of this coral island and into the unknown darkness, as if it was as easy to do as, to write about. He makes him straddle a strange island during a stormy night, and anchor witlessly at the end of the wrong one in the morning.

The circumstances in which St. Paul's ship approached an unknown island during a storm and darkness were different from those which Columbus found in the Bahamas, but the narrative of St. Luke, in the twenty-seventh chapter of the Acts, is instructive, because it shows an excellent piece of seamanship performed at land under great strain, by which, although the ship was lost, all hands were saved.[2] These ancient seamen had not learned to "bound along" the shores of unknown lands in a stormy night. Their thoughts at such a time were bent upon saving, not risking.

Captain Becher writes, 6th: That on the 19th of October Columbus went from the south end of Long Island to the northwest end of Crooked and remained on the west side of that and Fortune, until the 24th, when he sailed to the W. S. W., and on the 25th anchored, according to Captain Becher's chart, on the edge of "Columbus Bank," 19 miles E. ¾ N. from the South Ragged. Hence, on the 27th, he left for Cuba, steering S. S. W., and on the 28th brought his vessels to in the harbor of Nipe.

Page 131: Captain Becher speaks of the efforts which Irving and Humboldt made to establish Cat Island as the first landfall, in this way: "In reality they are so many proofs of the want of that patient and discriminate perusal of the journal which it really required."

Of his own work to the Crooked Island, he writes (pp. 154-155): "Thus far, then, among the islands which Columbus first discovered, he has here been traced by means of the courses he has given, the corresponding distances and relative positions of those islands from each other on the

---

[1] "The number of wrecks reported in 1858-'64 was 313, of which 259 were total losses."—*Report on the Bahamas for the year 1864*, by Governor R. W. Rawson.

[2] "*Voyage and Shipwreck of St. Paul*", by James Smith, London, 4th edition. Revised and corrected by Walter E. Smith; 1880, pp. 134-135.

chart, and the descriptions which he has left recorded concerning them with a degree of precision that places his position at any time beyond a doubt."

Pages 165–167: After arriving in Cuba he writes: "Señor Navarrete has recorded his opinion that this harbor is that now known as the port of Nipe. Following the Admiral to it, as has now been done, it cannot be any other. His track to it from the bank on which he anchored, the description which he has given of it, and the *deep channel* into it of twelve fathoms that no other near it possesses, clearly proves that Navarrete was right here when he declared that the port of San Salvador of Columbus in Cuba is in reality the port of Nipe. • • • It was necessary, in order to prove the identity of the landfall, to accompany Columbus from one island to another to compare as he went along his journal with the chart. • • • By the route through which the Admiral has been traced, his statements agree with the chart. The islands mentioned by him can be no other than those here pointed out. The track of the Admiral has been so clearly designated by himself, in direction at least, if not by the very compass point, as well as the distances he gives, which (with slight exceptions, to be attributed to blotted paper) so fairly correspond with those of the chart that the whole result deduced is at once conclusive and satisfactory. • • • A chain of evidence is completed from which there can be no appeal, and which establishes the real land-all beyond the reach of controversy."

Finally, speaking of Columbus's journal, Captain Becher writes (p. 174): "That it is not conformable to the ancient opinion of Cat Island being the landfall, but undoubtedly shows that Watling Island *was* that landfall, and in reality the island on which Columbus first landed in the new world. • • • If the island be now unquestionably pointed out. •. • • If his earliest footsteps in the new world • • • have now for the first time been successfully traced, the difficult task is amply rewarded by the harmony now established between the correct chart and the journal of Columbus, and in having finally set at rest the question of *the landfall.*"

ANSWER. From the south end of Long Island to Crooked and Fortune islands, hence toward the Sand Islands, Captain Becher's track is near to mine and will be referred to subsequently. Columbus did not anchor 19 miles E. ¾ N. of the Sand Islands (Ragged). His journal of October 26 reads: "He was on the *southern side* (1) of said islands; all was shallow for 5 or 6 leagues [15.9 to 19.1 nautical miles]. *He anchored there.*"(1)

I believe he did not go to port Nipe for the following reasons: From the mouth to one mile inside are these soundings in mid-channel, 39 fathoms, 35, 17, 28, 33, 17 and 18. See a Spanish plan published by the British Admiralty, October 25, 1826; corrected to 1855. The journal of October 28 reads: "The mouth of the river had 12 fathoms."

The course from the southern side of Sand Islands to port Nipe, is S. ¾ E. If the "two points of westerly variation," *supposed* by Captain Becher, be applied to the S. S. W. course steered by Columbus from the Sand Islands to Cuba, he would not have fetched it by three-quarters of a point, and there is a westerly current also to overcome.

The entrance to port Nipe looks east; it cannot be seen on a southerly course until one gets to it. A seaman would not run into a lee bight unless he was pressed, or acquainted with the land and knew of a harbor at the bottom. Columbus was probably running before the N. E. trades which made this bight a lee shore. His journal tells us that he went "to the land nearest to it" [him]. Such would be the act of a discoverer now. There are two harbors west of Nipe that come nearer to the words of Columbus's journal: Naranjo, with 13 fathoms at the entrance, and Padre with 14. Captain Becher might better have taken either.

The British Admiralty have begun to adopt the conjectures of Captain Becher on their charts, even to dividing the name of "Santa Maria de la Concepcion," which was given by Columbus. It must have come to pass from the positiveness of his assertions and not on account of his argumentation.

This method of applying Columbus's words in detail to refute each of the alleged tracks, and the study that I gave to the subject in the winter of 1878–'79 in the Bahamas, which had been familiar cruising ground to me, has resulted in the selection of Samana or Atwood Cay for the first landing-place. It is a little island 8.8 miles east and west; 1.6 extreme breadth, and averaging 1.2 north and south. It has 8.6 square miles. The east end is in latitude 23° 05′ N.; longitude 73°

---

(1) *Italics* are by the writer.

37′ west of Greenwich. The reef on which it lies is 15 by 2½ miles. On the southeast this reef stretches half a mile from the land, on the east four miles, on the west two, along the north shore one-quarter to one-half of a mile, and on the southwest scarcely one-quarter. Turk is smaller than Samana, and Cat very much larger. The selection of two so unlike in size shows that dimension has not been considered essential in choosing an island for the first landfall.(¹)

When Columbus discovered Guanahani, the journal called it "little island." After landing he speaks of it as "bien grande," "very large," which some translate, *tolerably*, or *pretty large*. November 20, 1492, Navarrete, first edition (p. 61), the journal refers to Isabela, a larger island than Guanahani, as "little island," and the 5th of January following (p. 125), San Salvador is again called "little island."

The Bahamas have an area of about 37,000 square miles, 6 per cent. of which may be land enumerated as 36 islands, 687 cays, and 2,414 rocks. The submarine bank upon which these rest underlies Florida also. But this peninsula is wave-formed upon living corals, whose growth and gradual stretch toward the south has been made known by Agassiz.

I had an unsuccessful search for a similar story of the Bahamas, to learn whether there were any probable changes within so recent a period as four hundred years.

The common mind can see that all the rock there is coral, none of which is in position. The surface, the caves, the chinks, and the numerous pot-holes are compact limestone, often quite crystalline, while beneath it is oolitic, either friable or hard enough to be used for buildings. The hills are sand-blown, not upheaved. On a majority of the maps of the sixteenth century there were islands on Mouchoir, and on Silver Banks, where now are rocks "awash"; and the Dutch and the Severn Shoals, which lay to the east, have disappeared.

It is difficult to resist the impression that the shoal banks, and the reefs of the Bahamas, were formerly covered with land; and that for a geological age waste has been going on, and, perhaps, subsidence. The coral polyp seems to be doing only desultory work, and that mostly on the northeast or Atlantic side of the islands; everywhere else it has abandoned the field to the erosive action of the waves.

Columbus said that Guanahani had abundance of water and a very large lagoon in the middle of it. He used the word *laguna*—lagoon, not *lago*—lake. His arrival in the Bahamas was at the height of the rainy season. Governor Rawson's *Report on the Bahamas*, 1864, p. 92, Appendix 4, gives the annual rainfall at Nassau for ten years, 1855–'64, as 64 inches. From May 1 to November 1 is the wet season, during which 44.7 inches fall; the other six months 19.3 only. The most is in October, 8.5 inches. Andros, the largest island, 1,600 square miles, is the only one that has a stream of water. The subdivision of the land into so many islands and cays, the absence of mountains, the showery characteristic of the rainfall, the porosity of the rock, and the great heat reflected from the white coral, are the chief causes for the want of running water. During the rainy season the "abundance of water" collects in the low places, making ponds and lagoons that afterward are soaked up by the rock and evaporated by the sun. Turk and Watling have lagoons of a more permanent condition, because they are maintained from the ocean by permeation. The lagoon which Columbus found at Guanahani had certainly undrinkable water, or he would have gotten some for his vessels, instead of putting it off until he reached the third island. There is nothing in the journal to indicate that the lagoon at Guanahani was aught but the flooding of the low grounds by excessive rains; and even if it was one communicating with the ocean, its absence now may be referred to the effect of those agencies which are working incessantly to reshape the soft structure of the Bahamas.

Samana has a range of hills on the southwest side about 100 feet high, and on the northeast another, lower. Between them, and also along the north shore, the land is low, and during the

(¹) I am indebted to T. J. McLain, esq., United States consul at Nassau, for the following information given to him by the captains of this port, who visit Samana or Atwood Cay. The sub-sketch on this chart is substantially correct: Good water is obtained only by sinking wells. The two cays to the east are covered with guano; white boobies hold the larger one, and black boobies the other; neither intermingle. The island is now uninhabited, but arrow heads and stone hatchets are sometimes found; and in places there are piles of stone supposed to have been made by the aborigines. Most of the growth is scrubby, with a few scattered trees. The Nassau vessels enter an opening through the reef on the south side of the island and find a very comfortable little harbor with from 2 to 2½ fathoms of water. From here they send their boats on shore to "strip" guano, and cut satin, dye woods, and bark.

season of rains there is a row of ponds parallel to the shore. On the south side a conspicuous white bluff looks to the southward and eastward. The two cays, lying respectively half a mile and 3 miles east of the island, and possibly the outer breaker, which is four miles, all might have been connected with each other, and with the island, four hundred years ago. In that event the most convenient place for Columbus to anchor in the strong N. E. trade-wind, was where I have put an anchor on the sub-sketch of Samana.

He did not note the direction of the wind while running for, nor when at Guanahani. I feel confident that it was the N. E. trade, since he gives the ~~speed of the vessels~~ from sunset ($5^h 41^m$) until 2 a. m. the next morning—October 11–12—as $22\frac{1}{2}$ leagues—$79\frac{1}{2}$ nautical miles—which is at the rate of $9\frac{1}{2}$ miles per hour, an unusual speed, and plainly indicating that he was running with a strong quartering wind under all sail, with fine weather. The "trades" generally freshen near the islands, but they are always in the eastern quarter. In the Bahamas they break up and are very light at east and southeast, but frequently blow strong when they get to the southward and westward, and the circuit ends with heavy squalls from the northward and westward; afterward north and northeast winds and fine weather prevail.

Columbus had none of the strong winds from a western quarter, because he was steering west. If the weather had not been fine he could not have seen the light at 10 p. m.—"like a small wax candle."[1] Neither could he have discovered the land at 2 a. m., 2 leagues—6.4 miles distant. *Varnhagen* (note I, p. 16) says the "moon shown bright, and a sailor saw by its light a white point; fired his lombard; called out land." I am greatly indebted to Professor William Harkness, United States Navy, of the Naval Observatory at Washington, for the moon's place. It was full October 5, O. S., 1492, at $10^h 58^m$ p. m., Greenwich mean time. It rose the 11th of October at 11 p. m., and at 2 a. m., when the land was sighted, it was 39° high, latitude 5° S., longitude 106° 03'. Those who were admonished by the admiral to keep a sharp lookout from the forecastle were, of course, looking ahead—west—and the moon, then nearly at the third quarter, was partly behind them and shone directly upon the white bluff. This was most favorable for seeing the land at night, and it is a memorable fact that Columbus first saw the New World through the light of the moon.

In the journal of the 14th of October the Admiral wrote that he "went along the island, in a north-northeasterly direction, to see the other side, which was on the other side of the east." The same date he said that in going along in the boats he "found a piece of land, like an island, although it was not one, with six houses on it, which in two days could easily be cut off and converted into an island." The first quotation is the language of a seaman who had anchored under a jutting point of land ~~which~~ stretched to the eastward and was in sight; he could see one side as far as the east end, but he desired to see the *other side of the east end.* Columbus was at anchor on an open coast; each vessel had but one boat, see Appendix E, and he took all the boats for his exploration of the 14th. For this reason, according to the usage of the sea, he ought not to withdraw far from his ships. The second quotation confirms the first, as to his being in the neighborhood of a peninsula. Both agree well with the east end of Samana. The point of land that Columbus said could easily be cut off has already been separated by the erosion of the waves. See sub-sketch of Samana.

It seems a weighty objection to Samana, that this name appears on the noted map of Juan de la Cosa, *together with* Guanahani. La Cosa was the companion of Columbus—seaman, chart-maker, pilot, master, and he made six voyages to the New World. It is said of him in *Disquisiciones Nauticas, por el Capitan de Navio,* Cesareo Fernandez Duro, Madrid, 1876, Tom. I, p. 59: "In the first voyage of Christopher Columbus, La Cosa went as master of his vessel, the same on which that officer served until it was wrecked in the Antilles: on the second he went likewise on board the caravel Niña styling himself master of chart-making, and in returning from this latter he was obliged to undertake in the port of Santa Maria the long and minute labor of making the chart which was finished in the year 1500." In 1832 Baron de Humboldt ~~and~~/Baron de Walckenaer found in the library of/~~the latter~~ an illuminated map skilfully drawn on an ox-hide. It measured 5 feet 9 inches by 3 feet 2 inches, was in good preservation, and bore the signature of La Cosa, and the

---

[1] Columbus met at Guanahani with canoes which held 45 men. The natives went in them as far as Cuba; they were fishermen and sailors, and the light of October 11 might have been in a canoe. Irving puts it on Watling; but Columbus was steering west, and if a line is drawn east, from the southeast point of Cat, Irving's landfall, it will go through the reefs north of Watling.

date 1500. A fac-simile was printed without notes, in Paris, from 1854–'60, for Jomard's work, titled *Les monuments de la géographie,* &c. Copies are in the principal libraries of the United States. This map has sustained the scrutiny and disputation of nearly a half a century, and the belief widens that it is the genuine work of Juan de la Cosa ([1]). The most suggestive figure thereon is Guanahani, since it has the same relative situation that Samana holds on modern maps; *both are little, narrow, east-and-west, outlying islands,* such as cannot be found elsewhere in the neighborhood. If La Cosa went with Columbus on the first voyage, he lay three days at Guanahani, and because he was "master of chart-making," his sketch of the first island should be true in respect to comparative size and exceptional position. A line drawn on the Appendix Chart, from the east end of Cuba, north a little easterly, to Samana, touches only Acklin, one of the Crooked Island group. A similar line drawn on La Cosa's map, reaches Guanahani by passing through one large roundish island marked Samana. Therefore, according to La Cosa, Samana was an *interior* island, *much larger* than Guanahani, *unlike* it in shape, situated near and in a southerly direction from it, about where Crooked and Acklin now are; whereas Samana on the present charts is applied to the little east-and-west island lying *outside* of the Crooked group. These facts and the disappearance of Guanahani from modern maps, led me to suspect and search for proofs of a transfer of this strange name of Samana.

Map of New Spain, by Nicolaus Vallard, of Dieppe, 1547: [reproduction by J. G. Kohl, in the library of the Department of State.] "Gamana" [Samana] is an interior island.

Theatrum Orbis Terrarum: Abraham Ortelius, Antwerp, 1572. Guanahany is an outside island and southwest of it, among others, is Samana.

Karte von Thomas Hood, *die Ostküste von Nordamerika bis zur Landenge von Panama,* 1592. Plate XIII. *Atlas zur Entdeckungsgeschichte Amerikas. Aus Handschriften der k. Hof- und Staats-Bibliothek etc.* Munich. Samana an interior and Guanahani an exterior island.

Descripcion de las Indias occidentales de Antonio Herrera, &c., Madrid, 1726—30, vol. 1, pp. 6–7: Here is a map of the Bahamas of the date of 1601, on which Guanahani is an exterior island, and to the southward and westward is Samana, an interior one.

Karte der Ostküste von Amerika von Neubraunschweig bis zum Amazonenstrome. Plate X of *Atlas zur Entdeckungsgesch. Am.* Munich. "Samano" [Samana] an interior island.

Carte du Mexique et de la Floride par Guillaume Del'Isle. Paris 1703. Samana, an interior island.

Map of North America, by John Senex, Charles Price, John Maxwell, geographers, 1710: The present group of Crooked and Acklin is marked "Samana or Krooked." Guanahani is a separate island.

An Accurate Map of North America. * * * *Also all the West India Islands,* by Eman. Bowen, Geographer to His Majesty; and John Gibson, engraver. 1733? I. Samana, Crooked, Fortune, and Acklin's form one group. Outside of these is *Atwood's Key.* This map is in vol. i *Old Maps of America,* No. 20. Library of Congress.

Atlas Historique, par Henri-Abrah. Chatelain, 7 vols. Amsterdam: In vol. vi (1738) the present place of Crooked group is marked "I. Samana."

d'Anville's Maps of 1731, 1746, *and* 1794: The present Crooked group is marked "Samana ou Krooked." Guanahani is a separate island.

G. Delisle and P. Buache. *Map of the Bahamas.* 1740. In a volume of maps, Library of Congress. I. Croqued, Fortune, and Acklin are strung along northwest and southeast. To the northeast of Croqued is a small island marked "I. Nova." It is near the present place of Samana. I have not met this name before. On page 80 of this volume is a map in which Samana appears as one of the Crooked Island group.

Bellin. 1750. Authority, J. Carson Brevoort, esq.: "Samana appears to be the northeast part of Crooked I."

Homann, Johannes Baptista, *Atlas Geographicus Major.* 2 vols. Nuremberg, 1759. Vol. i, p. 147. The present place of Crooked group is marked *Samana I.*

The West-India Atlas, by the late Thomas Jefferys, Geographer to the King. MDCCLXXV.

([1]) In *Sterene's Historical and Geographical Notes,* referred to farther on, the reader will find the objections to La Cosa's map satisfactorily answered.

Chart 8. The present Samana is marked "*el Terrigo or* Atwood's Key, *the Samana of the French.*" To the southwest is "*Samana or* Crooked Island."

Tour through the British West Indies, 1802–3, Dan'l McKinnen, London, 1804, p. 149: "Samana, spell Sumana, ancient Indian name of French charts; probably the original name of Crooked island."

These citations might be increased, but are they not enough to prove that the name of Samana has been shifted from an interior island, from the present Crooked group to the present Atwood Cay, thus surmounting a scholarly obstacle in the way of selecting Samana for the first landing-place? Columbus does not use this name. It appears first on La Cosa's map, for the island spoken of above, and also for the name of a bay on the northeast part of Hayti, which retains it now, but Columbus called it *Golfo de las Flechas: Navarrete,* vol. i, p. 139. An inquiry in regard to this name would be worth pursuing, but it does not belong to a discussion of the first landfall. On the 13th of October, the day before the Admiral left Gunnahani, he wrote: "I determined to wait until to-morrow evening, and then to sail for the southwest." This is all the information the journal gives in respect to the course steered *from* the first island. The inference is that he went as he said he should go, because he understood that *gold could be gotten in that direction.* But the proof shall be supplied by the subsequent agreements between the journal and the physical facts.

After he ~~had~~ left Guanahani he saw so many islands that he was undecided which to sail for first, but he determined to make for the largest. A vessel that leaves the east part of Samana and steers to the southward with some westing comes into view of the hills of Plana Cays, Acklin, and Crooked, on bearings from south-southeast to west by south, and to a stranger these hills would appear like so many islands. ~~After~~ Columbus anchored at the second island he wrote that it was five leagues, rather seven—15.9 or 22.3 nautical miles—from the first. The northeast end of Acklin bears S. W. by S. ¼ S., 23 nautical miles from the east part of Samana. For this discussion I consider Acklin and Crooked to be one island, under the name of Crooked. The channel which separates them is of modern origin, no doubt. It has the appearance of having been made by erosion; it is so shallow that it can be waded across, even at high water, and it is invisible to a passing vessel. See chart and sub-sketch.

Columbus wrote that the second island had a north-and-south side 15.9, and one east and west over 31.8 miles long. Crooked has a north-and-south side 13, and another which runs west by north and east by south 29 miles. A navigator of to-day could not come nearer to the truth, in describing the island in like circumstances; but Columbus kept his time with a sand-glass, and reckoned his speed by the eye. I wish the reader to take heed that it is the *second island, and no other,* of which the journal records the length and trend of two separate sides; and that *Crooked is the only one in the Bahamas* which conforms to this description.

A seeming objection to Crooked arises from the language in the journal of the 15th of October, that the side of the second island toward San Salvador ran north and south, whereas the side of Crooked which is in the direction of Samana runs east and west. Columbus could not note this fact at the first island, because Crooked is not visible from his anchorage there. After leaving Guanahani he saw many islands, and made for the largest. As he stood off and on all night, and the tide detained him on the 15th till about noon, he might have noted the side he then came to. This is the understanding of R. H. Major, who, in the *Journal of the Royal Geographical Society,* vol. xli, p. 198, translates the passage thus: "I found that the face of it, on the side toward San Salvador [or rather, I would suggest, on the side approached by the ships in coming from San Salvador], ran north and south five leagues, and the other side which I coasted ran east and west ten leagues."

From the data kindly supplied by the officers of the Naval Observatory in Washington, I learn that the moon crossed the meridian of Crooked Island on the 14th of October, 1492, at 6ʰ 36ᵐ a. m., Civil time. The British Admiralty Tide Tables for 1881 give VII o'clock for the "Establishment of the Port" at Crooked. Therefore it was high water there on the 14th of October at 1ʰ 36ᵐ p. m.; low at 7ʰ 48ᵐ, high at 2 a. m. on the 15th; low at 8ʰ 12ᵐ and high at 2ʰ 24ᵐ p. m. The sun set at 5ʰ 40ᵐ and twilight lasted about 1ʰ 19ᵐ. The journal does not give the wind *at* Guanahani, nor until the 16th, at the second island, when it is entered as S. E. I believe I have proved on p. 45 that Columbus made the land on the 12th of October with a strong N. E. trade; and the invariable circuit of winds alluded to on that page would give light easterly ones, sometime from the 12th to the 16th. During the regular "trades" the current between Samana and Crooked flows W. N. W. a knot an hour; but at other times the set and drift are uncertain. On the north side of Crooked the flood *tide* runs always to the eastward and the ebb contrarily. When Columbus neared the second island he estimated it to be 15.9 miles from the first; but the next day he called it 22.3. In the mean time he was detained by the *tide* so that he did not reach it again until about noon. Captain Becher (pp. 111–345) said that this detention was "set of the current"; but Columbus used the word *maréa*, not *corriénte;* the former signifies *tide,* flux and reflux; the latter *current,* progressive motion of the water; a distinction held in both languages and especially among seamen, and one of importance here.

These facts, in connection with the journal, enable me to offer a reasonable theory as to the movements of his vessels on the 14th and 15th of October. He left the south side of the east part of Samana on the 14th, undoubtedly after noon; and steered to the southward and westward, with light easterly winds, for Crooked. Midway he found the usual westerly current, and on the other side he ran into a stronger one setting in the same direction; but this was the *ebb tide* which flowed west, along the north shore of Crooked, from 1^h 36^m to 7^h 48^m p. m. He did not reach the land in time to see his anchoring-ground before dark, and the night was moonless. In consequence, he began, about sunset (5^h 40^m), to stand off and on; that is, he beat to the eastward to overcome this westerly set and keep his place until morning, when he intended to run in and anchor. At 7^h 48^m p. m. the tide turned and flowed east until 2 a. m. on the 15th. So that in the darkness of the night he had, unknowingly, six hours and twelve minutes of current, *contrary* to that for which he was allowing. In this way he got so far to the eastward that it was noon before he reached the island again; when he coasted the north shore and near sunset anchored at the west end. On the following day, the 16th, he wrote his journal of the 15th, by which time he had observed the distinction between the currents and tides in the neighborhood of Crooked, and he noted the one which caused his detention.

The second island of Columbus has been such a stumbling-block to investigators that many of them assert that he sighted it, but passed on without stopping. See translation from Muñoz, *ante,* p. 36, and discussion with Captain Becher, *ante,* p. 37. Major (p. 198) wrote: "Here I beg to call your attention to the fact that Columbus neither lands upon nor gives any name to the first island which he reaches after leaving Guanahani, a fact which argues its unimportance and sanctions our assuming it to be Rum Cay." The weight of these authorities makes it necessary for me to try to answer them before I go on. The following paragraph from the Spanish text of the journal is the authority upon which Major and Captain Becher found their assertion that Columbus did not land upon the second island (Navarrete, 1st edition, p. 25, October 15, and *ante,* p. 25): "*Y como desta isla vide otra mayor al Oueste, cargué las velas por andar todo aquel dia fasta la noche, porque aun no pudiera haber andado al cabo del Oueste.*" Major's translation (p. 198) is: "And as from this island I saw another larger one to the west, I started for the purpose of sailing the whole of that day until night, for otherwise I could not have reached the westernmost cape." Captain Becher (p. 109) renders it: "And as from this island I saw another larger one to the westward, I made sail, continuing on until night; for as yet I had not arrived at the western cape." Mr. Thomas's translation, which I have adopted, is: "And as from this island I saw another larger one to the west, *I clewed up the sails,* for I had gone all that day until night, because I could not yet have gone to the western cape." The essential difference is with, *cargué las velas.* Major makes it, "I started"; Captain Becher, "I made sail"; and Thomas, "I clewed up the sails." In *Diccionario Maritimo Español,* etc., *por D. José de Lorenzo, D. Gonzalo de Murga y D. Martin Ferreiro, Empleados en la Direccion de Hidrografía,* Madrid, 1864, the definition agrees with that given by Mr. Thomas. So of all other Spanish dictionaries which I can find. I have also submitted the phrase to Spanish officers with like result. The signification is, to clew up, or brail up; that is, take in sail. A similar expression occurs in the first part of the journal of October 15: "I had been standing off and on this night fearing to approach the shore for anchorage before morning not knowing whether the coast would be clear of shoals, and intending to clew up—*cargar velas*—at dawn." If he had been hove to all night he might have written "I will make sail in the morning"; but as he was standing off and on, the two clauses—"Fearing to approach the shore for anchorage before morning," and "Intending to clew up at dawn", are connected, and the meaning of *cargar velas* in the latter is obviously to take in, not to make sail.

The proof that he stopped at the second island does not depend upon the signification of any one phrase, but upon the concord existing between the journal and the cartographic facts. Columbus promised in his Prologue (see Appendix D) that he would mark "each night my progress during the day and each day the run made during the night.' But it can be readily understood that he had no regular time for writing his journal among the Bahamas, where the navigation is difficult and where the Indians thronged upon him as coming from heaven. This appears upon reading the remarks under October 11, the day before seeing Guanahani. All the journal of that day—with the exception of the first forty-seven lines—refers to transactions which took place on the 12th, a date omitted from the journal. From the closing paragraph of the 13th it seems that most of his Guanahani log was written near sunset of that day. He says: "At this moment it is dark and all went on shore in their canoes." The 14th was written in the afternoon, during the leisure which came to him from being at sea, clear of the land and the inhabitants. He wrote then: "I looked for the largest one and determined to make for it, *and I am so doing*."(¹) It is important that I should call attention to the fact that all the journal of the 15th was certainly written on the 16th. He entered no remarks on the 15th. Under this date, which was Monday, he wrote: "I anchored and remained until *to-day Tuesday*(¹) when at dawn I went on shore with the boats armed." Same date, farther on, 15th, he writes: "And soon after I set sail for the other large island." He could not have done so except on the 16th, the day he wrote this. His story in the journal of the 15th is certainly the experience of the 16th. For example: near the close of the remarks of the 15th he writes: "And being in the Gulf midway between these two islands namely that of Santa Maria and this large one, to which I give the name of la Fernandina." No one can fail to see that this circumstance, and those immediately preceding it, belong to the 16th, although found under date of the 15th. His journal of the 16th begins with the statement that he left Santa Maria for Fernandina about noon, an assertion repeated twice on the 15th, but which could not have been put into execution until the 16th. A study of the journal of the 15th and 16th shows that his first leisure was the afternoon of the 16th, in the calm weather between the two islands, and *then* he wrote the journal of the 15th. That of the 16th was not written until the 17th, for he writes under the former date about sending the ship's boat on shore for water at 9 a. m.—certainly on the 17th. A little later in the journal of the 16th he says: "Soon after writing this I set sail with a south wind." As he did not arrive at the island to which this refers until the morning of the 17th, see first part of the journal of this day, it is obvious that it was of the 17th—not the 16th—that he was speaking. The student who is attentive to the journal will notice that Columbus wrote it when he could find time—to all appearance at one sitting, as a very busy sailor would do. This led him often to set down the matter of several days under one date, and he seems not to have overhauled his log to see whether it was at variance with itself.

Remembering, then, that all the things done on the 15th were recorded on the 16th—after he had left the second island—they might be put into a concise and truthful statement as follows: Columbus explored Guanahani in the boats before noon of the 14th, and sailed after noon to the southward and westward, the direction of the gold. Many islands coming shortly into sight, he made for the largest, but did not reach it in time to see the anchoring-ground before dark. The wind being light from the eastward, and a strong current running west, he decided to stand off and on, or beat to the eastward, to hold his position during the night, that he might anchor in the morning *at that part of the island which he had seen before dark*. The next forenoon, the 15th, he found himself so far to the eastward that it was noon before he got back. He observed two sides of the island, one north and south, five leagues; the other, east and west, over ten. He approached the first, but as it was a lee-shore he followed the other all the afternoon, arriving at the western cape about sunset, whence he saw another large island to the west. Not wishing to be under weigh again at night, among the tides and currents, and the wind having canted to the southward and eastward, which gave him a weather shore to anchor under, he clewed up his sails and came to. On the morning of the next day, the 16th, he went on shore to explore the island, but, as the wind increased from the S. E., and his ships were riding to a weather tide, they were liable to be set

_____
(¹) *Italics* by the writer.

across it and foul their anchors: *ante*, p. 16, note 2. The Admiral observing this from the shore, returned and weighed anchor before or at noon, for the island in the west.

Major, p. 198 (*ante*, p. 47), and Captain Becher, pp. 108–112 (*ante*, p. 37), admit, what is obvious in the journal, that Columbus steered for the second island on the afternoon of the 14th, stood off and on during the night, and the following day he was detained by the tide or current until noon, when he reached this second island, and *then* he followed that side of it which ran east and west over ten leagues, and came to anchor at sunset, 5ʰ 40ᵐ.

My interpretation is that he did not go beyond this second island on the 15th, but that he anchored about sunset at the west cape of the side he had followed. This would make his run 10 leagues—31.8 nautical miles—in 5ʰ 40ᵐ, equal to 5.6 miles each hour. Major and Captain Becher say that, in addition to coasting this side, he kept on eight leagues—25.5 nautical miles—farther, where he came to anchor at sunset, making a sum of 18 leagues—57.3 nautical miles—in 5ʰ 40ᵐ, which gives a speed of 10.1 nautical, or 12.7 Italian, miles for every hour—greater than is recorded anywhere for his vessels. He must have had a gale of wind all the afternoon of the 15th to have been driven at such extraordinary speed; but there is no mention of it in the journal. His log across the Atlantic was 105¼ nautical miles a day, equal to 4.4 miles every hour. The best day's run was October 4, 200.5 nautical miles, an average of 8.4 each hour.

Columbus wrote on the 14th of October, in respect to the second island: "I looked for the largest one and determined to make for it, and I am so doing." On the 15th—written on the 16th and relating solely to past events—he said: "It was about noon when I reached the said island. • • • The other [side] which I followed ran east [and] west, and contains over ten leagues. And as from this island I saw another larger one to the west, I clewed up the sails for I had gone all that day until night [noon to sunset], because I could not yet [otherwise] have gone to the western cape, to which I gave the name of Santa Maria de la Concepcion, and about sunset I anchored near said cape in order to learn whether there was gold there." This is the island of which Columbus wrote, in his letter to Santangel (*ante*, p. 38): "To the second island I gave the name of Santa Maria de Concepcion." It lay in the direction of the gold; it was the largest in sight; the Guanahani Indians reported, "That they there wore very large rings of gold on their legs and arms." Columbus wrote that one island taken possession of, the same may be said of all; but it was his desire not to pass any without taking possession, and he did not. After sailing from this island he wrote: "And being in the gulf midway between these two islands namely that of Santa Maria and this large one, to which I gave the name of *Fernandina*," he found a man in a canoe who had come "from the island of San Salvador, had passed to Santa Maria, and was now going to a Fernandina," the very sequence he was doing. All who are mindful of these facts from the journal of the 14th, 15th, and 16th of October, may group them better than this to suit their own mind, but in every aspect they will outweigh the assertion that he did not stop at that second island which he made for on the 14th, and strove for on the 15th.

Columbus anchored at the northwest cape of Crooked (Santa Maria), at sunset, October 15, and waited there until the following forenoon. He wrote: "And as from this island I saw another larger one to the west, I clewed up the sails." It would appear from this paragraph that the island referred to came into view when he reached the west cape, near sunset. Writing of what took place the next day, he said: "I set sail for the other large island that appeared at the west." He begins the 16th with, "About noon I left the *islands of Santa Maria de la Concepcion* for the *island of Fernandina*, which appears to be very large to the west." Long Island lies 25 miles west of Crooked, and the range of hills upon it, marked 150 feet high, are two miles farther. The distance of visibility for 150 feet is 14 miles, and for Columbus's lookout, of 60 feet, it is 8.8 miles; total, 22.8 miles. In consequence Long Island cannot be seen from Crooked.

I have alluded, on page 44, to probable physical changes among the Bahamas in the past, but I shall not appeal to these here. Seamen understand very well that, in favorable circumstances, the appearance of land is very striking over coral islands which are below the range of visibility from the observer. This is especially noticeable in the Bahamas, because all the necessary conditions are there: low islands of white coral; not enough trees or undergrowth to hinder radiation; a high degree of heat, and the air loaded with moisture. When a fall of temperature happens this is precipitated into a cloud cap which often covers the island like a blanket, and outlines it. It is this and the blending of cloud and land that makes the latter appear, frequently, to be above the horizon when truly below it. (¹)

Columbus sailed from the northwest end of Crooked, October 16, either at 10 a. m. or noon, for he gives both times, toward the island which appeared in the west. Calm weather retarded him until daylight of the 17th, when he anchored at a cape of an island, which he named Fernandina. Here, he said, the coast ran north-northwest and south-southeast. On the way over he estimated the distance from the second to the third island at nine leagues. After he had arrived he called it eight leagues—25.5 nautical miles. A course from Crooked W. ¼ N. 25 miles strikes a cape of Long Island where the coast line runs as given by Columbus. See chart and the sub-sketch of Long Island, the latter on a larger scale, which shows the cape and trend of land more distinctly. The appearance of Long Island (Fernandina) from Crooked (Santa Maria), the course and distance between them, the southeast cape and the trend of the coast of Long Island (Fernandina), all conform accurately to the facts and we need not linger upon them.

At noon of the 17th of October, Columbus sailed from this southeast cape, steering along the shore to the N. N. W., "the wind being S. W. and S." When he was near the end of the island "two leagues off" he found a marvellous port with two entrances formed by a rocky islet in the middle. Both were narrow, but within was ample room for 100 ships, if there had been sufficient depth free from obstructions, with a deep entrance. He was so much impressed with this marvellous port that he anchored outside of it and went in with all the boats and sounded it and saw that it was too shoal. This was the first opening into the land that he had met with and he thought it betokened a fresh-water river, therefore he took in the water casks. His former visit to a tropical country was to Guinea (Africa) where all the openings in the shore are made by fresh-water streams.

The wind was off the land, and he remained in this harbor with the boats, getting water, for two hours, when he returned to the vessels and sailed. Columbus wrote that the entrance of this marvellous port was two leagues from the end of the island. The reader will observe how often the journal uses leagues and miles in such a way that an interchange of them was possible on the Admiral's part and very probable with the copyist.(²) If the two leagues of the journal were a clerical error for two Italian miles, it corresponds with the chart. See sub-sketch of Clarence Harbor, where the southeast entrance is two Italian miles (1.6 nautical miles) from Booby Cay, the visible extremity of the island; and the course to the latter is N. W. He wrote that he sailed on this course until he discovered that part of the island which ran east and west; and afterward the Indians persuaded him to go back, and because the wind ceased and then sprang up from the W. N. W., which was contrary to his course, he turned around. This and the subsequent courses point out that he was following this east-and-west shore on a likely course of W. N. W. when the wind came out ahead. After turning around he sailed all night, E. S. E., sometimes E. and also S. E. to clear the land. He wrote that the atmosphere was very misty and the weather threatening, but that the wind was light and it did not permit him to reach the land to anchor, and that it rained hard after midnight until almost day. He adds, "We [are] at the southeast cape of the island where I hope to anchor until it gets clear." He closes the journal of the 17th with general remarks, which was his frequent habit. It is evident that he wrote this paragraph, and the last observations of the 17th, on the morning of the 18th, at the southeast cape of the island, where, as he was exposed to rainy weather and light winds, he desired to anchor.

(¹) Since I navigated among the Bahamas a light-house has been built at the N. W. end of Crooked, and I wrote to T. J. McLain, esq., United States consul at Nassau, asking him to inquire from officials merely whether Long Island could be seen from it. This is his answer: "I saw Capt. W. H. Stuart, who has commanded the light-house yacht Richmond for many years, and who is a most trustworthy person. He agreed to look up the matter and get me reliable information. The Richmond returned lately from a trip to the windward light-houses, and the captain called to-day to report. He says he inquired particularly of both the keepers at Bird Rock Tower, and of Mr. Arauha, who is clerk of the board of works at that station, and the three united in saying that Long Island is *not* visible from Bird Rock light-house, that they have never seen it, even on the clearest day. A gentleman residing near there says he has seen smoke on it in a clear day. And all four say that they have frequently seen clouds settle over Long Island in still weather *like a stretch of land*. [*Italics* by G. V. F.] Captain Stuart says that all his own observations confirm the foregoing statements."

(²) *Navarrete*, vol. i, p. 101, December 21, 1492: On this day he was at the present bay of Acul on the north side of Hayti, and the journal reads: "The distance from the entrance to the bottom of it [Acul] is about five leagues." This is a clerical error for five miles, because the bay of Acul is 25,800 feet deep, equal to 5¼ Italian miles.

These words imply that he was at the cape from which he had sailed the day before. In other words, that he had retraced his steps as he was advised to do, and getting back to a familiar anchorage, with unfavorable conditions for coasting such shores, he wished to anchor and wait for clear weather.

On page 49 I have asked the student to take heed in adapting the dates in Columbus's journal. The caution is necessary here. The log of the 18th of October opens with a clause which belongs to the remarks quoted above; for he says: "After it cleared up I followed the wind"; the last of this date is, "At dawn I set sail." It is enough to read the journal of the 19th, which was written in the evening of this day, *after arriving* at the rocky islet, to see that getting under way at dawn of the 18th referred to the same act done at dawn of the 19th. What he did on the 18th is not obscure; shifting tides and inconstant winds hindered him from following the coast to a favorable anchorage. This appears from his remark on the 18th, I "went around the island as much as I could, and I anchored when it was no longer possible to sail."

We find recorded in the journal certain physical characteristics concerning the second island which belong to Crooked only; and in like manner is the third island established. This is so important that I briefly recapitulate. Columbus anchored at a cape of the third where the coast line was north-northwest and south-southeast. He followed it N. N. W. until he came to a marvellous port, two leagues [miles?] from the end. He sounded it in the boats and found it capacious, but shallow. He sailed N. W. until he opened that part of the shore which ran east and west; he steered along it W. N. W. till the approach of night and the advice of the Indians caused him to turn about.

A sailor describing the strange things seen in new lands is likely to put into his *story* some of the warmth of his vocation, but not in his log. When he enters the course steered, the depth of water, the trend of the coast, and the speed of his vessel, these are facts which his daily duty calls for, and the safety of his ship may turn upon the accuracy of the record. Columbus's description of the shore-lines and harbor of the third island relate to physical facts which he observed. They are his log, and they cannot be ignored. It is essential, therefore, that a third island shall be found answering to this description. The sub-sketch on the chart shows at a glance that the southeast part of Long Island is the only land and water that will fit. See narrative of Captain Becher 17th and 18th of October, *ante*, for the entanglement arising from using another island for the track of these two days.

There is an element of time here which is important as it limits the ground passed over on the afternoon of the 17th. The Admiral left the southeast cape at noon and turned around while heading W. N. W., and then he steered an opposite course during the night, to clear the land. It is fair to select sunset, $5^h 40^m$, as the time of his turning. As long as he could see the land and reefs he might keep on, but *not after dark*. He would choose the day only to explore new shores. In the night he might retrace his steps steering well off, or anchor, or heave to, or stand off and on, nothing else. The distance from the southeast cape past the shallow port and around to the end of the east-and-west side is 22 nautical miles. As he stopped at the above port two hours, he was under way only $3^h 40^m$. This gives a speed of 6 miles an hour, which is fully as much as his vessels were likely to do. Any track which is longer, or which requires more speed than this, must be very liable to error.

If Columbus turned at sunset on the 17th and returned to the southeast cape at "almost day" of the 18th he sailed in a night which had ten hours of darkness, the distance he went over in $3^h 40^m$ of day. This is not strange. In addition to the various courses steered to clear the land, he says, of this night, that the atmosphere was misty and the weather threatening, but *the wind light*. The fact that he followed this shore at all during such a moonless night is proof that he had gone along it the day previous and learned the direction of the shores, so that he retraced his steps without much hazard *provided he steered well off*. This he could do; for in coasting the island the afternoon before he must have observed that there was no land on the other side to pick him up.

Columbus is now at anchor on the southwest side of the south end of the third, or Long Island (Fernandina). He sailed from here at dawn on the 19th. Sunrise was at $6^h 21^m$, twilight $1^h 19^m$, dawn at $5^h 2^m$. The flag-ship steered S. E., the Pinta E. and S. E., and the Niña S. S. E. Three hours had not elapsed when they saw an island to the east for which all the vessels headed, and before mid-day they arrived at the northern extremity, where there is a rocky islet. I take this to be the north end of Fortune Island. See chart and sub-sketch of Crooked Island anchorages. The Admiral gives no distances in sailing across. If he was fairly under way at 5ʰ 30ᵐ and anchored at 11ʰ 30ᵐ, the time was 6 hours, half of which he steered S. E. and half E., making E. S. E. if each three hours was equal speed. From the south end of Long Island to the north end of Fortune the course and distance are E. by S. ¾ S. 32 nautical miles. This gives a little more than 5.3 miles an hour, which is fair sailing for his vessels. Columbus wrote on the evening of the 19th that this rocky islet "lay from the island of Fernandina, whence I had come east [and] west, and the coast afterwards ran from the rocky islet to the westward, and there was in it twelve leagues." If the last clause is an error for 12 Italian miles, it agrees with the chart, as the coast inclines from here two points to the west and measures 10.5 nautical miles, or 13.2 Italian miles.

Long Island is invisible from the rocky islet, and the line between them is not east and west. In steering from Fernandina Columbus spread his vessels from an E. to a S. S. E. course, to get hold of the land; then he drew them together on one course and afterward anchored. A bearing entered at this time with reference to an island no longer in sight, and from which they had arrived by steering several courses, might easily be 1¾ points in error.

Fortune is the fourth island of Columbus's visitation, the one he named ~~after~~ that manful and lovable queen, *Isabela*, who sent him on his way when kings and councils rejected him. It will be noticed that the journal makes the third island lie west of the second, and the fourth east of the third. This brings the second and fourth adjacent to each other, as they are found upon the chart. If a landsman thinks that the Admiral ought to have known that the land now north of him was the same which lay south on the evening of the 15th, it can be ~~truly~~ answered, that one of the most perplexing things in the vocation of the sea is the recognition of lands or islands that have no conspicuous marks. Light-houses, beacons, and pilotage grew out of this difficulty. Columbus sees the *opposite side* of Crooked, after an interval during which he was harassed by navigating the shores of the third island. He comes in sight of it for the second time, while steering a course opposite to that which he steered at first; and of all islands to distinguish, none from the other, or the different sides, the Bahamas are the most puzzling, owing to their similarity. *Irving*, vol. i, p. 433, wrote of the Admiral: "On his second voyage returning from Cuba, he coasted the southern side of his favorite island of Haiti without recognizing it until a cacique came off and addressed him by his title and used several words of Castilian. The news spread joy throughout the ships." The mountains of Haiti are 9,000 feet high and are easily recognized now, for we know their height and have excellent maps; but Columbus was making discoveries where the islands seemed to be innumerable; he was not surveying, nor had he any instruments by which he could lay down accurately the relative bearings of the lands.

The first part of the journal of October 20 remarks upon the failure of the vessels to get to the eastward of Isabella, either by the northeast or south, on account of shallow water. This agrees with the present cartography of Fortune Island. My position here derives strength from a statement in the journal of November 20. *Navarrete*, p. 61: On this day the Admiral was 25 leagues—79.6 nautical miles—N. E. ¾ N. from Puerto del Principe, admitted to be the present Cuban port of Tanamo. The appendix chart has the 20th of November laid down at 75 miles only, arising from the use of 3 as a multiplier for leagues, instead of 3.1818. The Admiral said that on this day he was 12 leagues—38.2 nautical miles—from Isabella. From here to Fortune Island, which I call Isabella, the distance is 36 miles; but to Great Inagua, Navarrete's Isabella, there are 60 miles; to Long Island, Irving's Isabella, 67, and to Crooked, selected by Captain Becher, 53. The journal adds that he could have anchored at Isabella, but did not wish to, for fear that the Indians he had brought from Guanahani might escape, as the distance between these two islands was but eight leagues—25.5 nautical miles. Fortune is 36 miles from Samana; Crooked and Watling, the Isabella and Guanahani of Captain Becher, are 68 miles apart; Grand Turk and Great Inagua, the Isabella of Navarrete, are 101.

At the beginning of October 24 Columbus sailed from the rocky islet, at the north end of Fortune, on a predetermined W. S. W. course. The day was characterized by rain, calms, little wind, and then a "lovely" breeze. At nightfall, 5ʰ 30ᵐ, the southwest cape of Fernandina (Long Island) bore N. W. distant 22.3 miles. This is known at sea as "departure." The night of the 24th–25th he had strong winds with rain, and being on unknown ground he first reduced, then took in all sail. He said he had made much headway, of which he was doubtful, but he estimated that he did not go this night two leagues. The direction of the wind is not noted. He says that it grew strong suddenly, with mist and rain. Such wind and weather are well known among the Bahamas; they are the sudden rain squalls which are common from the northward and westward (ante, p. 45.) At sunrise on the 25th he made sail at W. S. W., but at 9 a. m. he steered west—no doubt to make the former course good, which he had lost somewhat in the night, by drifting under bare poles.

At 3 p. m. the Admiral saw land. "There were seven or eight islands, all extending from north to south; distant from them five leagues," 15.9 nautical miles. He anchored on the 26th of October in the shallow water south of these, which he called Sand Islands. The course and distant from the rocky islet to the south sand island are W. S. W. 82 miles. The same from the "departure"—night-fall of October 24th—W. S. W. 65 miles. The journal gives the following distances between "departure" and Sand Islands: Night of the 24th-25th, not two leagues. Five leagues to 9 a. m. on the 25th. From 9 to 3 p. m., 44 miles, and then 5 leagues to the Sand Islands. Ten leagues, 44 Italian miles, are 66.8 nautical miles. This accord between the log and the truth, on the largest run the Admiral made in the Bahamas, is not accidental. In the journal of the 23d-24th, we see that he is disappointed with the poverty of the land and people, and his ardent temperament seizes upon what the Indians called Cuba, to signify that land of gold and spices and large ships for which he had sailed from Spain—Cipango (Japan). He carefully notes the direction to it, pointed out by the natives, who would be most likely to indicate the way their canoes went, touching at intermediate land. He believes this course is W. S. W., and to make it good he would put forward all his skill.

About 60 miles N. N. E. of the northeast coast of Cuba, a line of cays and islands extend N. N. W. ½ W. and S. S. E. ½ E. for 21 miles. The principal ones are eight : Nurse, Bonavista, Racoon, Double Breasted, Maycock, Hog, Great Ragged, and Little Ragged. From the southernmost a coral bank stretches 28 miles south, and 30 east, having from 4 to 11 fathoms of water, interspersed with rocky heads and shoal spots. This is known as the "Columbus Bank"; it terminates the Great Bahama Bank on the southeast. Here, then, is the fifth island, or islands, visited by Columbus; and it should be noted that such a string of islands, and bank of shallow water stretching from them, described so correctly in the journal, cannot be found anywhere else in the Bahamas.

He left this anchorage Saturday, October 27th at sunrise (6ʰ 23ᵐ) and steered S. S. W. for Cuba. By sunset (5ʰ 37ᵐ) he had made 17 leagues—54.1 nautical miles—about 4.8 knots an hour. He saw the land before dark, but kept off "on the look-out during the night with much rain." Sunday he resumed his course S. S. W., striving to reach the nearest land. Arriving there he entered a beautiful river which had 12 fathoms at the mouth. The courses "logged" from the Sand Islands are S. S. W., and the distance 54.1 miles, which was made by sunset Saturday. In the night he probably held his position. Sunday he again steered S. S. W., but as the time of anchoring is not given, we do not know how much more was made on this course. It is certain, only that the distance from the Sand Islands to this Cuban port was more than the run to Saturday night, 54.1 miles. If he anchored early Sunday, which is probable from the soundings and explorations he made on this day, it did not exceed it but little.

Columbus designated this beautiful river and port with his favorite title, San Salvador. This name has not been preserved, and each investigator points out his own choice. I select Port Padre. The course and distance on this chart, from the Sand Islands, are S. W. ¼ S. 63 miles. Some authorities place Padre ten miles farther west, in which case it would be S. W. ¼ S. 71 miles. The currents here are thus spoken of in the West India Pilot, vol. i, p. 6: "Sometime the current on the north coast of Cuba as far west as Matanzas runs one to four knots to the westward." The vessels of Columbus were under its influence from Saturday afternoon until he entered the river, and as I allow no variation to the compass (see Appendix C), his true course should be as much to the west of S. S. W. as the current drifted him. Port Naranjo answers the description of the journal as well as Padre, but it is S. ¾ W. 62 miles from South Ragged, and a vessel could not, of course, get to it steering S. S. W. with a westerly current. I choose Padre because it is the only port west of Naranjo that has depth of water enough at the mouth to satisfy the journal, and in other respects is free of objections. See Sheet II, Harbors and anchorages on the north coast of Cuba, from a Spanish plan, U. S. Hydrographical Office, 1876, which gives the soundings of Port Padre. Outside are 8½ fathoms; at the entrance, 14; then 8, 6, 10, and 9, through to the harbor.

As a matter of interest, I have laid down a track for the vessels of Columbus from Padre west, as far as Boca de Guajaba, where he probably turned. He then coasted the northeast shore of Cuba, crossed to Hayti, and followed the north side to the present bay of Samana, where his first voyage in the New World ended. This track coincides, sometimes, with the track of Navarrete, but both are liable to be inaccurate, owing to the imperfection of the charts of the north coast line of Cuba and Hayti.

Washington Irving lays so much stress upon Herrera's description of the voyage of Ponce de Leon through the Bahamas that I am constrained to examine its merit at the hazard of making this paper wearisome to the reader. The translation from Herrera is in his *Columbus*, revised edition, vol. i, pp. 378–379: "Leaving Aguada in Porto Rico they steered to the N. W. by N. and in five days arrived at an island called El Viejo in latitude 22° 30′ N. The next day they arrived at a small island of the Lucayos called Cayeos. On the eighth day they anchored at another island called Yaguna in 24°, on the eighth day out from Porto Rico. Thence they passed to the island of Manuega, in 24° 30′, and on the eleventh day they reached Guanahani, which is in 25° 40′ N. This island of Guanahani was the first discovered by Columbus on his first voyage and which he called San Salvador."

Irving remarks upon this that the latitudes are placed too high, but that the substance is conclusively in favor of Cat Island. He says Ponce de Leon's first island, El Viejo, must have been Turk's Island. This agrees with the old maps. The second he thinks was one of the Cayeos. There can be no doubt of it. The third, he says, was probably Mariguana. But Herrera gives the third as Yaguna; and by the old maps this appears to be the present Inagua. Irving calls the fourth island Crooked; Herrera's fourth is Manuega, considered by scholars to be that now known as Mariguana. The fifth island Irving says is Isla Larga (Long Island), and lastly Guanahani. This would make Guanahani the sixth, but the narrative ~~above~~ gives only five islands touched at.

It seems more reasonable to believe that Ponce de Leon left Aguado and steered N. 49° 18′ W. 287 miles to El Viejo (Grand Turk). The next day he ran over to one of the southerly Cayeos cays some 30 miles to the southward and westward. He arrived on the eighth day at Yaguna, probably Little Inagua, 75 miles to the westward of his last place. Thence he steered to the northward 55 miles to Manuega (Mariguana), the fourth island since leaving Porto Rico. From Mariguana his next stopping-place is Guanahani. Herrera writes that on the eighth day out Ponce de Leon was at Yaguna (Little Inagua), and on the 11th at Guanahani, having touched at Manuega (Mariguana) on the way. This gives three days from Yaguna (Little Inagua) to Guanahani, including one anchorage at Manuega (Mariguana). The distance is 108 miles from Little Inagua to Samana, touching at Mariguana. The same to Watling is 176, and to Cat 213.

Ponce de Leon was five days from Porto Rico to Grand Turk, 287 miles, equal to 57.4 miles a day, on a straight course, clear of the land and within the "trades". If we use this distance to measure his run from Little Inagua to Guanahani—and we have no other—then these two islands were three days apart, 172.2 miles. But he stopped at Manuega (Mariguana) on the way, so we can only reduce this distance by guess. But the less the distance the greater the probability that Guanahani was, in the opinions of the contemporaries of Columbus, an island *not far from Manuega* (Mariguana). If Ponce de Leon left Little Inagua, touched at Marignana, and then anchored at Samana (Guanahani), the sequence is apparent and the distance, 108 miles in three days, including one stop, is fair. But to Cat, 213 miles in the same time, would be greater speed than in any other part of the voyage, and there are several large intervening islands where he was likely to anchor, as he did between Aguado and Manuega (Mariguana).

Herrera was the official historiographer of the Indies in the sixteenth century, ~~and he~~ had ~~exclusive~~ access to the original documents of Columbus and other explorers. Therefore he is a good witness to cite against the assertions in favor of Grand Turk and Mariguana. If Ponce de Leon sailed *from* each of these islands *to* Guanahani, neither can be the first landfall of Columbus in the view of this historian.

CONCLUSION.

There is a common belief that the first landing-place is settled by one or another of the authors cited here. Nevertheless, I trust to have shown, paragraph by paragraph, wherein their several tracks are contrary to the journal, inconsistent with the true cartography of the neighborhood, and to the discredit, measurably, both of Columbus and of Las Casas. The obscurity and

56

the carelessness which appear in part of the diary through the Bahamas offer no obstacle to this demonstration, provided that they do not extend to the "log" or nautical part.

Columbus went to sea when he was fourteen years of age, and served there almost continuously for twenty-three years. The strain of a sea-faring life, from so tender an age, is not conducive to literary exactness. Still, for the very reason of this sea experience, the "log" should be correct. This is composed of the courses steered, distances sailed over, bearings of islands from one another, trend of shores, &c. The recording of these is the daily business of seamen, and here the entries were by Columbus himself, chiefly to enable him on his return to Spain to construct that nautical map which is promised in the prologue of the first voyage.

In crossing the Atlantic the Admiral understated to the crew each day's run, so that they should not know how far they had gone into an unknown ocean. Las Casas was aware of this counterfeit "log," but his abridgment is from that one which Columbus kept for his own use.

If the complicated courses and distances in this were originally wrong, or if the copy of them is false, it is obvious that they cannot be "plotted" upon a correct chart. Conversely if they *are* made to conform to a succession of islands among which he is known to have sailed, it is evident that this is a genuine transcript of the authentic "log" of Columbus, and, reciprocally, that we have the true track, the beginning of which is the eventful landfall of October 12, 1492.

The student or critical reader, and the seaman, will have to determine whether the writer has established this conformity. The public, probably, desires to have the question settled, but it will hardly take any interest in a discussion that has no practical bearing, and which for its elucidation leans so much upon the jargon of the sea.

It is not flattering to the English or Spanish speaking peoples, that the four hundredth anniversary of this great event draws nigh, and is likely to catch us still floundering, touching the first landing-place.

SUMMARY.

First. There is no objection to Samana in respect to size, position, or shape. That it is a little island, lying east and west, is in its favor. The erosion at the east end by which islets have been formed, recalls the assertion of Columbus that there it could be cut off in two days and made into an island. The Nassau vessels still find a snug anchorage here during the N. E. trades. These blew half a gale of wind at the time of the land-fall; yet. Navarrete, Varnhagen, and Captain Becher anchored the squadron on the windward sides of the coral reefs of their respective islands, a "*lee shore*." (See the chart.) The absence of permanent lagoons at Samana I have t.ied to explain on p. 44.

Second. The course from Samana to Crooked is to the southwest, which is the direction that the Admiral said he should steer "to-morrow evening." The distance given by him corresponds with the chart.

Third. The second island, Santa Maria, is described as having two sides which made a right angle, and the length of each is given. This points directly to Crooked and Acklin. Both form one island, so fitted to the words of the journal as cannot be done with any other land of the Bahamas.

Fourth. The course and distance from Crooked to Long Island is that which the Admiral gives from Santa Maria to Fernandina.

Fifth. Long Island, the third, is accurately described. The trend of the shores "north-northwest and south-southeast"; the "marvellous port" and "the coast which runs east [and] west," can nowhere be found except at the southeast part of Long Island.

Sixth. The journal is obscure in regard to the fourth island. The best way to find it, is to "plot" the courses *forward* from the third island, and the courses and distances *backward* from the fifth. These lead to Fortune for the fourth.

Seventh. The Ragged Islands are the fifth. These he named *las islas de Arena*—Sand Islands. They lie W. S. W. from the fourth, and this is the course the Admiral adhered to. He did not "log" all the run made between these islands; in consequence the "log" falls short of the true distance, as it ought to. These "seven or eight islands, all extending from north to south," and having shoal water "six leagues to the south" of them are seen on the chart at a glance.

Eighth. The course and distance from these to Port Padre, in Cuba, is reasonable. The westerly current, the depth of water at the entrance of Padre, and the general description, are free of difficulties. The true distance is greater than the "logged" because Columbus again omits part of his run. It would be awkward if the true distances from the fourth to the fifth islands, and from the latter to Padre, *had fallen short* of the "log," since it would make the unexplainable situation which occurs in Irving's course and distance from Mucaras Reef to Boca de Caravela (*ante*, p. 36).

From end to end of the Samana track there are but three discrepancies. At the third island (*ante*, p. 21) two leagues ought to be two miles. At the fourth island (*ante*, p. 23) twelve leagues ought to be twelve miles. The bearing between the third and fourth islands is not ~~quite as~~ the chart ~~has it~~, nor does it agree with the courses he steered (*ante*, p. 23). These three are fairly explained, and I think that no others can be mustered to disturb the concord between this track and the journal. (1)

In this paper I mention only the publications containing what was indispensable to the discussion. The student who is eager to sift the matter further will derive much aid by searching among the following:

Bartlett, John Russell. *Bibliographical notices of rare and curious books relating to America, printed in the XVth and XVIth Centuries (1482–1601) in the library of the late John Carter Brown, of Providence, R. I.* Providence, printed for private distribution, 1875.

Harrisse, Henry. *Bibliotheca Americana Vetustissima:* a description of works relating to America, published between 1492–1551. New York, 1866.

——— [*idem:* containing additions.] Paris, 1872.

Rich, Obadiah. *A catalogue of books, relating principally to America*, arranged under the years in which they were printed. London, 1832.

——— *Bibliotheca Americana Nova;* or a catalogue of books in various languages, relating to America, printed since the year 1700. Parts I, 1701–1800, and II, 1801–1844. London, 1846.

——— *Bibliotheca Americana Vetus:* Books relating to America, 1493–1700 [also] Supplement. London, 1846.

Stevens, Henry. *Historical and geographical notes on the earliest discoveries in America:* 1453–1530 [with] fac-similes of many of the earliest maps and charts of America. New Haven and London, 1869.

Winsor, Justin. *Columbus; a bibliographical note from the catalogue of the Ticknor collection.* Boston Public Library, Bulletin No. 10, 1876.

I acknowledge my indebtedness for intelligent help to—

The Superintendent and assistants of the United States Coast and Geodetic Survey.

H. L. Thomas, esq., translator of the United States State Department.

Rear-Admiral John Rodgers, United States Navy, Superintendent of the United States Naval Observatory, and his assistants.

A. R. Spofford, esq., Librarian of Congress.

J. Carson Brevoort, esq., of Brooklyn, New York.

T. J. McLain, esq., United States consul at Nassau, New Providence, Bahamas.

Capt. J. C. P. de Krafft, United States Navy, hydrographer to the Bureau of Navigation, Navy Department, and his assistants.

Commander Juan N. Montajo, Royal Spanish Navy.

Professor Pedro Montaldo, Instructor in Spanish at the United States Naval Academy.

W. H. Tillinghast, esq., graduate of Harvard University, class of 1877.

Woodbury Lowery, esq., M. A., of Harvard University, class of 1875.

Theodore F. Dwight, esq., of the State Department.

Prof. A. M. E. Elliott, of Johns Hopkins University.

I am also grateful to the Navy Department for assistance, and to the following libraries for invaluable facilities: the Library of Congress, and of the State and of the Navy Department in Washington, the Lenox and Astor Libraries in New York, and the Library of Harvard University in Cambridge.

(1) La Cosa's map preserves the name of Guanahani instead of San Salvador. It is evident that this sturdy old seaman was heedful of the fixed names. There are obvious and strong reasons for saving enchorial names from obliteration. In this case *Guanahani* is the oldest American name we have. It is all that remains from the wreck which the white man made of this gentle race. If ever there shall be any agreement upon Samana, for the first landing-place, I hope that the name of *Guanahani* may be restored to it.

APPENDIX A.

AGE OF COLUMBUS.

The range of years ascribed to his birth is from 1435–'36 to 1446–'47.

For 1435–'36 are Bonnefoux, Irving, Bernaldez, Napione, Navarrete, Humbolt, and Luigi Colombo.

For 1441, Charlevoix.

For 1445, Cladera and Bossi.

For 1446, Muñoz.

For 1447, Spotorno and Robertson.

For 1446–'47, see *Select Letters of Columbus*, 2d edition, by R. H. Major, introduction, pp. xxxii–xxxiv.

If he was born in 1435 his age was fifty-seven when he discovered the New World; if in 1447 he was forty-five.

Without attempting an investigation of the question, I refer to the following exploit of Columbus as bearing upon it, Irving's revised edition of *Columbus*, vol. i, pp. 28–29:

"The first account of his being engaged in a naval expedition was one fitted in 1459 by John of Anjou, Duke of Calabria, to make a descent upon Naples to recover that kingdom for his father. It lasted [this struggle] four years [until 1463]. During this expedition Columbus was detached on a perilous cruise to cut out a galley from the harbor of Tunis. Columbus himself relates that when he arrived off San Pedro, in Sardinia, he heard that there were two ships and a carrack with the galley, by which information the crew refused to go on, and determined to go to Marseilles for reenforcements. Columbus apparently acquiesced, but altering the compass-card he so deceived them as to arrive off Tunis instead of Marseilles."

Columbus wrote to King Ferdinand (Major, introduction, p. xxxvi): "It happened to me that King René (whom God has taken to himself) sent me to Tunis to capture the galley Fernandina," &c. If the king sent him on this hazardous and independent enterprise during the last year of the expedition to Naples—1463—he was only sixteen years of age, if born in 1447. The naval profession will not admit that any authority, either ancient or modern, would intrust to a boy of sixteen the execution of a deed likely to put to the proof the ability of an able and efficient seaman.

If we take 1435–'36 for the year of his birth—and there the weight of authority lies—he was twenty-seven to twenty-eight when he went to Tunis, and fifty-six to fifty-seven when he landed on Guanahani. It is more reasonable to believe that he was fifty to fifty-one, rather than thirty-nine to forty, when he offered his plan to the king and queen of Spain; and under all the circumstances of his tedious solicitation, that he could not have been fewer than fifty-six to fifty-seven years of age when he saw the New World.

APPENDIX B.

MILE AND LEAGUE OF COLUMBUS.

In *Navarrete*, 1st edition, vol. i, p. 258, Columbus wrote: "56⅔ miles to an equinoctial degree."

Page 300, fourth voyage: "The world is not so large as the common opinion makes it, one degree of the equinoctial line measuring only 56⅔ miles."

Page 3, August 3, 1492: "Steered southward until sunset under a strong sea-breeze, making 60 miles, which are 15 leagues."

On pp. 3–4 is this note of Navarrete: "Columbus used Italian miles, which are shorter than the Spanish, thus four of the former and three of the latter make a league."

I notice that writers multiply the leagues of Columbus by 3 and call the product a geographical mile. My search for accuracy, and to see where the multiplier 3 was obtained, is not conclusive. Rear-Admiral John Rodgers, superintendent of the United States Naval Observatory, after giving the subject some investigation, is of opinion that the ancient Roman or Italian mile was 1,614 English yards. An article in the *Penny Cyclopedia* (Mile and League) written by Augustus De Morgan, late professor of mathematics in University College, London, calls the ancient Italian mile 1,614 English yards. Humboldt discusses the subject of leagues, miles, and degrees in his *History of the New Continent* (note, vol. ii, p. 216) without bringing their length to any undisputed measure. So with Pigafetta *Treatise on Navigation*, p. 216.

Martin Cortes, *Breve Compendio de la Sphera, &c.*, Seville, 1551, English translation, 1561, folio xix, has this table :

    4 grains of barley make a finger.
    4 fingers a hand or palm.
    4 hands a foot.
    5 feet a geometrical passus.
    2 steps make a passus.
    125 passus a furlong, or stadium (old English furlongs long)([1]).
    8 furlongs one mile.
    1 mile is 1,000 passus.
    3 miles one league; in Germany longer leagues;
       France, 15 leagues to one degree;
       Spain, 16¾ leagues *and* 17½ *for a degree of the Great Circle.*
Pedro de Medina, *Arte de Navega*, Valladolid, 1545, prefers 4 miles to a league.
Pigafetta says, " shore leagues 3 miles ; nautical, 4."

On the 9th of December, 1492, Columbus was at the present Bay of Acul, Hayti. The journal reads *Navarrete*, vol. i, p. 84 : *Este puerto tiene en la boca mil pasos, ques un cuarto de legua*— " The harbor here is about a thousand paces, or a quarter of a league wide at the mouth." It is evident that with Las Casas 4,000 "pasos" was a nautical league. By using the table above and the note below, this league is found to be 20000.64 English feet.

Since the Italian mile of Admiral Rodgers and Professor De Morgan is 1,614 yards, or 4,842 feet, and Columbus called four of these a league, this was 19,368 English feet, which differs only 632.64 feet from that derived from Las Casas's remark and Martin Cortes's table.

In the computations of this paper the mile of Columbus is 1,614 yards or 4,842 English feet, and his league 6,456 yards or 19,368 English feet. For the geographical or nautical mile or knot, I have adopted Clarke's estimate of one minute of arc on the equator, rejecting a small decimal. This is 2,029 yards or 6,087 English feet. Where there is an omission to designate the kind of mile this is the one meant. I have tried to prove these measures by comparing them with some of the distances given in the journal, but the result is unsatisfactory. Allowing 3 leagues de, parture from St. Sebastian (Gomera), he sailed, according to his log, 1,111 leagues to Guanahani-= 1178.33 of Clarke's leagues, or 3,535 nautical miles, 3,458 on a straight course. Cat Island is the farthest landing ascribed to him. It is 3,141 miles from Gomera, an overrun of 317 miles. The Grand Turk is the nearest, 2,834 miles ; a difference of 624.

In Dr. Chanca's narrative of the second voyage of Columbus, *Navarrete*, vol. i, p. 200, the distance sailed from Ferro to the first land, Dominica, is called 800 leagues, 2545.5 nautical miles. The true distance is 2,529. He remarks that it is 300 more between Ferro and Cadiz, equal to 954.6 nautical miles, but the true distance is 774.

([1]) *Modern Metrology*, by Jackson, London :

Page 41. " The present value of the English furlong adapted to the English statue mile—a modern arrangement—is 132 paces, but as the old London mile of 1,000 paces was the local form of the Roman mile, its former value was 125 paces."

Page 66. " Old London mile = 1,000 paces = 5,000 feet = .9470 mile"—of 5,280 feet. This would make the old London mile 5000.16 English feet.

December 5, 1492, the journal has 120 leagues—381.8 miles—for the distance he coasted Cuba. From Boca de Guajaba, where he probably turned, to Cape Maysi, the coast line is 244 miles. In giving a summary of his first voyage to Luis de Santangel, Navarrete, vol. i, p. 168, Columbus wrote that he followed the coast of Cuba for 107 leagues—340.5 miles—and the coast of la Española for 178 "grandes leguas." If these are like the other leagues they equal 566.3 miles. The true distance, along the coast-line of Hayti, between St. Nicolas Mole and Samana Bay, is 286 miles. Andres Bernaldes, *Mass. Hist. Col.*, vol. viii, 3d series, p. 6, said that Columbus went 88 leagues—280 miles—in a straight line from west to east, along Hayti. The navigator of these shores still finds the same currents and baffling winds; but he is spared such errors of distance, because of the perfection of chronometers and of nautical instruments.

Columbus was very correct in estimating the short runs. He called it ten leagues from Navidad to Isabella, on the north side of Hayti. This is the true distance. Considering the guess-work in the distances among the Bahamas, he was surprisingly accurate, as I have shown in the discussion.

Taking the mile of Columbus at 4,842 feet, his estimate of the circumference of the globe was 16227.3 nautical miles. Clarke's circumference, at the equator, is 21,600 nautical miles, each 6087.11 English feet. The earth was larger around by 33 per cent. than Columbus believed.

APPENDIX C.

VARIATION OF THE COMPASS IN 1492.

In Captain Becher's *Landfall of Columbus*, Appendix, p. 331, is this: "In laying down the track of Columbus from the Crooked Island group, named in the chart the Fragrant Isles, from the journal of the Admiral, it becomes evident from his courses and distances, run as far as Cuba, that it was necessary to allow a considerable amount of variation. In his first voyage he mentioned in his journal that he found above a point of westerly variation, on a meridian a hundred leagues west of the Azores, and in his third voyage, when he is on the coast of Paria, he also mentions having found, to the surprise of the pilots, above a point and a half. And now that his courses and distances run to an anchorage in the bank specified as being at the distance of five leagues from the Arena isles, and from thence to Cuba, it may be safely said that the variation which he found there in 1492 amounted to little short of two points westerly."

All that Columbus wrote in respect to the deviation of the needles referred to his observations on the Atlantic during his first voyage. *Navarrete*, 1st edition, vol. i, p. 8, September 13, 1492, Thursday: "On that day, at nightfall, the needles northwested, and in the morning they north-wested somewhat;" page 9, September 17, 1492, Monday: "The pilots [mates] took the north [star] marking it, and found that the needles northwested a full point, and the sailors feared and were troubled, but did not tell why. The Admiral was aware of it, and ordered that they should again mark the north [star] at dawn, and they found that the needles were all right; the cause was that the star which appears moves and not the needles;" p. 15, September 30, 1492, Sunday: "NOTE.—That the stars called las guardias([1]), at nightfall, are close to the arm in the west, and at dawn they are in the line below the arm to the northeast, so that it seems that during the whole night they do not advance more than three lines, or nine hours, and this every night: this is what the Admiral says here. Also at nightfall the needles northwest one point, and at dawn they are with the star exactly; from which it appears that the star moves as do the other stars, and the needles always demand the truth;" p. 254: in the letter of Columbus to his sovereigns, giving a narrative of his third voyage: "I remarked that from north to south in traversing these hundred leagues from said islands [one hundred leagues west of the meridian of the Azores], the needles of the compass, which had hitherto northeasted, northwested a full point of the compass, and this took place from the time when we reached that line;" and p. 256: "For in sailing thence one hundred leagues west of

---

([1]) Guardias—name given to two of the most brilliant stars of the constellation Ursa Minor. Dominguez, *Spanish Dictionary*.

the meridian of the Azores the ships go on rising smoothly toward the sky, and the weather was felt to be milder on account of which mildness the needle shifts one point of the compass, and the farther we went the more the needle northwested, this elevation producing the variation of the circle which the north star describes with las guardas." These last two extracts were written during his third voyage, but they refer obviously to what took place on the *first*.

On the 13th September, 1492, Columbus had run 227 leagues—722.3 miles—due west from Gomera, when he discovered that the compasses had westerly variation. By the 17th he had gone 136 leagues—432.2 miles—more on the same course, when the observation of the pilots showed a full point west variation. At dawn, however, under the direction of the Admiral, they again took the bearing of the north star and found that the needles were "all right." The abridger does not give the words of the Admiral, he interprets them, and they are hardly intelligible. Could Columbus have tampered with the compass-card to allay the fears of his crew, as he did at Sardinia to get his vessel to Tunis (Appendix A)? By September 30 he had sailed 295 leagues—940.2 miles—additional; total run from Gomera of 2094.7 miles west, during which he had made but four miles of southing.

In the letter of Columbus to his sovereigns, quoted above, we have his own words, clear enough as to the deviation of his needles, but not in regard to the cause. He wrote that they changed from easterly to westerly on a meridian one hundred leagues—318.2 miles—west of the meridian of the Azores, and thence west the variation increased the farther he went. The meridian of the Azores is, probably, that of Corvo, the most western one. The southeast end is in latitude 39° 41′ north, longitude 31° 07′ west from Greenwich.

Captain Becher has evidently taken for granted that by the time Columbus got to the Crooked Islands, which are 972 miles west a little south, of the position of September 30, the deviation had gone on increasing so as to be "little short of two points westerly." Columbus went four times to the West Indies, but he never mentions any deviation there. As already stated, he refers to the northwesting of the needles *in the Atlantic Ocean* after he had crossed the meridian of the Azores.

If the variation alleged by Captain Becher is applied to Columbus's courses across the Atlantic his track would go south of the Bahamas. Captain Becher steers Columbus S. W. from Watling to Rum Cay. Two points west variation will take a vessel, at least, six miles east of it. He steers him west from the north shore of Rum Cay to the northwest end of Long Island. Two points west variation would put the vessels on shore eleven miles southeast of the cape. From Bird Rock to the anchorage on Columbus Bank, where Captain Becher anchors Columbus, the course is S. W. by W. But Captain Becher, pp. 160, 161, says that Columbus steered W. S. W.; so *here* he let him have one point only of west variation, and yet he anchors him 19 miles too far to the eastward. If he had given him the two points he says should be allowed here, the vessels would have made S. W., clearing the bank and going out of sight of the "Sand Islands." Columbus anchored *south* of these islands (South Ragged). From there Port Nipe bears S. ⅞ E.; a course S. S. W., allowing two points west variation, would not fetch it by three-quarters of a point; and, in addition, there would be the strong westerly current to allow for. It is probable that Captain Becher got his variation from Ferdinand's *Discovery of the West Indies by Christopher Columbus*. The original of this narrative is lost, and the various versions have no standing among scholars where the statements are unsupported. In an English translation, *Collection of Voyages and Travels by Churchill;* London, 1732, vol. ii, p. 587, is this: "Yet the Admiral says he could not from this time give such an account as he would wish, because through overmuch watching his eyes were inflamed and therefore he was forced to take most of his observations from the sailors and pilots. He also says that this same night, being Thursday, the 16th of August [1498], the compasses which till now had not varied, did at this time, at least a point and a half, and some of them two points, wherein there could be no mistake because several persons had always watched to observe it. Admiring at this and grieved that he had not the opportunity of following the course of the continent, he held on N. W. till on Monday, the 20th of August, he came to an anchor between Benca and Hispañiola." These alleged observations were taken near the island of Margarita, on the coast of Paria. They are worthless on their face, because, without moving, the variation went from nothing to two points. Ferdinand refers to the *third voyage* of his father; but above I have quoted Columbus's own words of the same voyage, from his letter to the king and queen, in which he is not speaking of the variation *on the coast of Paria*, but of that he found *on the Atlantic* during his *first voyage*.

The compass-cards used by Columbus were divided into points, instead of points and quarters, as now. Sights for taking bearings were not introduced until the next century. It appears from the journal, that he depended upon the north star to find his variation. In 1492 the polar distance of this star was 3° 28′; now it is 1° 20′. There is no doubt but that he used the astrolabe and compass to get its bearing, but the difference of 5° and 10°, *Navarrete*, vol. i, p. 255, proves that accurate observations for variation were impossible in 1492. His course across the Atlantic, worked from his log, with no variation allowed, is W. 2° 49′ S. The course from Gomera to Turk Island is W. 8° 1′ S. Conceding that he landed at this the most southern island ascribed to him, he made 5° 12′ southing, which might have been due to the southwest current, that is is constant between the Canaries and West Indies, rather than to west variation. The courses from Samana or Atwood Cay to Cuba have no allowance for variation.

When Columbus, on the 5th of December, 1492, stood across from Cuba to Nicolas Mole, Hayti, he gave the course S. E. by E. If he started from an offing of 4½ miles to the northeast of Cuba, given on this chart, the true course is S. E. ⅓ E. If he steered S. E. by E., he would be set as much as three-quarters of a point to the southward by the current which flows S. W. in the "Windward passage."

August, 1498—third voyage—Columbus sailed from the west side of Margarita Island for the city of St. Domingo, in Hayti. The true course and distance are N. 35° W. 594 miles, but he brought up at Beata, 110 miles west of this city, N. 46° 24′ W. 558 miles from Margarita. He ascribed his falling to leeward solely to the current; Irving's *Columbus*, revised edition, vol. ii, p. 124.

The equatorial current in the Caribbean Sea sets always to the westward; on the coast of South America it is 1½ to 2 miles an hour; in mid-sea, about one mile, or about an average of one mile each hour to a vessel standing across. He was five days making the passage (120 hours), during which he was set to the west 110 miles. On his last voyage he fell to leeward also in crossing this sea, and it was almost fatal to him. Nowhere does he attribute his westing to any cause but the true one—*currents*. If the compass was flying about as Ferdinand wrote, or if there was any deviation in the West Indies worth noticing, a seaman as accurate as Columbus in noting physical things should have recorded it.

Expressing my doubts of the correctness of Captain Becher's allowance for variation to the Superintendent of the United States Coast and Geodetic Survey, he called upon his assistant, Mr. C. A. Schott, for a scientific examination of the subject. The result was a paper written by him, dated April 8, 1881, which will appear in the report of the United States Coast and Geodetic Survey for 1880, appendix 19. Mr. Schott's deductions are that the deviation in 1492 in the Bahamas did not exceed one-quarter of a point west.

For the reasons stated here I have allowed for no deviation of the needle on any course in 1492.

APPENDIX D.

THE LOG OF COLUMBUS ACROSS THE ATLANTIC OCEAN, 1492.

Las Casas's abridgment of this is in the first volume of *Navarrete*, pp. 1–166. Columbus said, in his prologue: " I have decided to write daily and minutely everything that during that cruise I should do and see and how much I should run. * * * In addition to the marking each night my progress during the day, and each day the run made during the night, to construct a new chart," &c.

Pages 3–4: " We left Friday, 3d day of August, 1492, from the bar of Saltes at 8 o'clock; we steered under a strong sea-breeze until sunset to the south sixty miles, which are fifteen leagues; afterwards southwest and south by west, which was the course for the Canaries."

I am informed that the Spanish naval service reject days of the week, and use those of the month only, and that their sea day begins at noon of the civil day. Until 1847 the English and United States naval service kept the usual civil day in port, but at sea the day began at noon, twelve hours before the civil day.

It is not clear what day Columbus used. His prologue seems to refer to the ancient sacred day of the Jews, or that of the Church, beginning at sunset. The Athenians, Chinese, Italians, and others reckoned by this. Reading, carefully, all his log, I find days which might furnish arguments for his use of the present civil day, or that he might have counted either from noon to noon or sunset to sunset. In this paper I shall consider that he used the present way, midnight to midnight. The island of Gomera, from which Columbus sailed, is 14 by 11 miles, nearly a round mass of mountain, rising to 4,400 feet. The harbor of St. Sebastian lies a little south of the east end, and by "Bowditch's Navigator" is placed in latitude 28° 6' north, longitude 17° 8' west from Greenwich. After he left this port he was becalmed until Saturday night, when the first course "logged" is W. Since some departure must be allowed to clear the land, I have put down 3 leagues S. W. ¼ W., barely enough to enable him to begin a W. course. I do not know whether he went south or north of Gomera; I make his course south, because the prevailing winds there are from the northward and eastward.

The most western island of the Canaries is the one called Hierro by the Spanish, and Ferro by the Portuguese. The parallel of 27° 44' north, and the meridian of 18° west from Greenwich, pass through the middle of the island. This was the "prime meridian" from Ptolemy until the last century. Hierro is 34 miles S. W. by W. ¼ W. from Gomera. Columbus left St. Sebastian Thursday morning, September 6, 1492. "Directing his course for the voyage * * * he was becalmed all day and night." * * *

September 7: "The whole of Friday, and on Saturday until three hours after nightfall, he was becalmed." * * *

September 8: "On Saturday three hours after nightfall it began to blow from the northeast, and he resumed his course to the west," &c.

His voyage began three hours after sunset—about 9ʰ 36ᵐ p. m.—Saturday, September 8. The following are the dates, courses steered, and distances:

Date.	Courses.	Distance in leagues.	Remarks.
September 6 to 8, allow	S. W. ¼ W.	3	This is the allowance for departure.
September 8	West	0	His predetermined course.
Sunday, September 9	....do	40	
10	....do	60	4 ?
11	....do	40	? .
12	....do	33	
13	....do	33	?
14	....do	20	
15	....do	27	
Sunday, September 16	....do	39	?
17	....do	50	6 .
18	....do	55	.
19	....do	25	1 ?
20	W. by N	7.5	Baffling winds and calms.
21	West	13	
22	W. N. W.	30	Contrary wind.
Sunday, September 23	{ N. W.	....	Some calm and high sea.
	{ N. W. by N	....	
	{ West	22	
24	West	14.5	
25	{ West	4.5	Steered S. W., supposing he saw land.
	{ S. W.	17	
26	{ West	16	
	{ S. W.	15	Same reason for going S. W.
27	West	24	
28	....do	14	
29	....do	21	

Date.	Courses.	Distance in leagues.	Remarks.
Sunday, September 30	West	14	
October 1	....do	25	
2	...do	39	
3	...do	47	
4	...do	63	
5	...do	57	
6	...do	40	
Sunday, October 7	West	23	
	W. S. W	5	Steered W. S. W. because flocks of birds flew in that direction.
8	W. S. W	11.5	
9	S. W	6	
	W. by N	5	
	W. S. W	29.5	Baffling winds.
10	W. S. W	50	
11	W. S. W	27	
	West	17	Changed his course to west at sunset; gives no reason for it.
Friday, October 12	West	5.5	
	..do	2	Discovered land at 2 a. m., two leagues distant.
		1,111	Columbus's leagues.

Allowing for the detention by calms in the Canaries, departure, and difference of time, he was 33½ days from Gomera to Guanahani.

In the above log I have not copied his daily remarks during the voyage, for they have no bearing upon this discussion. I have, however, noted that he never deviated from his predetermined west course, unless constrained by head winds, baffling winds, or the strong appearance of land to the southward and westward. And the student will take notice that, notwithstanding the observations in regard to the westerly variation, on the 13th, the 17th, and the 30th of September, the Admiral did not alter his courses in order to make true west, but that he held firmly to *west by compass.*

The following is an abstract or "traverse table" of his courses and distances across the Atlantic:

Courses by compasses.	Columbus's leagues.	Nautical leagues.	Nautical miles.	Difference of latitude.		Departure.	
				N.	S.	E.	W.
S. W. ½ W.	3	3.2	9.5	....	6	....	7.3
West.	882.5	936	2,808	....	....	....	2,808
W. by N	12.5	13.3	40	7.8	....	....	39.2
W. N. W.	52	55.1	165.5	63.3	....	....	152.9
S. W.	38	40.3	121	....	85.6	....	83.6
W. S. W.	123	130.4	391	....	140.4	....	361
Total	1,111	1,178.35	3,535	71.1	241	....	3,454

If this table is worked out by "Mercator's Sailing," in "Bowditch's Navigator," which is not so accurate as "plotting" each day on the chart, but is near enough for practical purposes, then his course and distance, by dead reckoning, are W. 2° 49′ S., 3,458 nautical miles.

From Gomera to Grand Turk the course and distance are, W. 8° 1′ S., 2,834 miles; Gomera to Mariguana, W. 6° 37′ S., 3,032 miles; Gomera to Watling, W. 4° 38′ S., 3,105 miles; Gomera to Cat, W. 4° 20′ S., 3,141 miles; and from Gomera to Samana (Atwood's Cay), W. 5° 37′ S., 3,071 miles.

He overran the distance between Gomera and Grand Turk by 624 miles; Gomera and Mariguana by 426 miles; Gomera and Watling by 353 miles; Gomera and Cat by 317 miles; and Gomera and Samana by 387 miles. These overruns might have been due to the current between the

Canaries and the West Indies, which always sets to the southward and westward in mid-ocean, and more westerly, near the West Indies. It varies from 9 to 30 miles per day, according to the force of the trade-winds.

It increases our estimate of the determined spirit of Columbus that he "logged"—*believed that he had actually made*—3,535 miles directly into the "Sea of darkness," exceeding by 500 miles the distance between New York and Liverpool.

In 1492 latitude was found by meridian altitude of the sun, or by the north star.

Major, introduction, p. li, has it, that about 1480, "by the joint labors of Martin Behaim and the Prince's two physicians, Roderigo and Josef, * * * the astrolabe was rendered serviceable for the purposes of navigation, as by its use the seaman was enabled to ascertain his distance from the equator by the altitude of the sun."

Humboldt's *Cosmos*, translated by Otté, London, 1849, vol. ii, p. 670 : "The astrolabe described by Raymond Lully, in his *Arte de Navegar*, was almost two hundred years older than that of Martin Behaim." Second volume of Cosmos, p. 630, he speaks of Martin Behaim's invention as "perhaps only a simplification of the meteoroscope of his friend Regiomontannes."

Bossi's Columbus, 2d edition, Paris, 1825, p. 151 : "The astrolabe received in the 13th century its form which made it universally used. Andelone del Nero, of Genoa, wrote upon it, and published it at Ferrara, in 1477."

Chaucer's treatise on the astrolabe, 1391, edited by Walter W. Skeat, London, 1872, p. xxiv, says that it was well known in India and Persia, by the Arabs, and spoken of by *Marco Polo.* On p. xxxiii is a description of its powers, among which are the latitude of any place by two observations of the pole star, or any circumpolar star, or sun's meridian altitude; can be used to discover approximately the four cardinal points of the compass, and in what part of the heavens the sun rises, &c.

The longitude was gotten by "dead reckoning." The speed of a vessel was estimated by the eye. There is no mention of the "log-line" until the next century.

The time was kept by the "sand-glass."

APPENDIX E.

THE VESSELS OF COLUMBUS.

Very little is known in regard to the vessels that took the first discoverers to the New World. Clark's *Maritime Discoveries*, vol. i, p. xxvii: "The chief characteristics of ships of Da Gama's age (close of the fifteenth and beginning of the sixteenth century) were height of poop and prow, squareness of lower yards, taunt masts, and small round tops."

In Churchill's *Collection of Voyages and Travels*, London, 1732, vol. ii, is Ferdinand Columbus's history (narrative) of the discovery of the West Indies by his father. On p. 586: "The Admiral durst proceed no farther in his ship, which required three fathoms water, being of a hundred tun." This refers to the date of August 10, 1498, third voyage, off the coast of Paria. *Irving's Columbus*, revised edition, vol. i, p. 123: "Peter Martyr, contemporary of Columbus, says: Only one was decked, built up high at the prow and stern, with forecastles at the prow and cabins at the stern."

Columbus's journal, October 11 : "The Admiral at 10 o'clock at night standing on the castle of the poop;" farther on, he "requested and admonished them to keep a sharp lookout at the forecastle." In the *History of the Catholic Sovereigns, Ferdinand and Isabela*, by Bernaldez, an extract of which is printed in the *Massachusetts Historical Collections*, vol. viii, third series, pp. 52–53 : "They found themselves in only 2 fathoms of water; * * * the vessels being often aground. * * * They found 2 fathoms and a cubit(¹) of water and room for the caravels to remain, and they anchored." These extracts refer to the second voyage of the Admiral, when he was among those many islands on the south side of Cuba, which he called the "Queen's Gardens." On this voyage he had three large ships and fourteen caravels; but in February, 1494,

(¹) Cubit is generally stated to be 18 English inches—old Paris foot=12.789. F. A. P. Barnard, in *Johnson's Universal Cyclopædia.*

App. 18——9

he sent twelve back to Spain, from Navidad, and he pursued his voyage with the caravels (small vessels), as mentioned by Bernaldez. A. Jal, *Archéologie Navale*, Paris, 1840, vol. ii, p. 237: "Tonnage of vessels of the fifteenth century voyaging to the Canaries were 90 tuns (about), supposes a length of keel of 70 to 80 (French feet)[1]." On p. 229 he deduces the length and breadth of Columbus's vessels, first quoting from *Las Casas's Narrative in Navarrete*, vol. i, p. 70: "Tuesday 27th, 9th month, 1492. This mouth of a stream was of the breadth of 5 (brasses French) brazas, which was in dimensions the length of the boat." Then he adds: "A boat of 5 brazes would suppose a vessel of 27^m 77^c total length, and 8^m 12^c amidships, according to Venetian treatise in Memoir 5."

On referring to *Navarrete*, p. 70, November 27, 1492, we find the following to be the true rendering of the day Jal speaks of: "After the vessel had anchored the Admiral jumped into the boat in order to sound the port, which is like a small porringer; and when he was opposite the mouth at the south he found an entrance to a river which was so wide that a galley could enter therein, and in such a manner that it was not seen until it was reached, and entered into at about one boat's length it had five fathoms and eight in depth."

Fincham's History of Naval Architecture, p. 34, date referred to, 1498: "Cabot * * * was authorized to take six ships out of any haven in England, of the burthen of 200 tuns and under."

Page 44: "The largest of Drake's vessels, 1577, was the Pelican of 100 tuns burthen."

Review of the Laws of Tonnage, by G. Moorsom, London, 1853, p. 1: "Whatever was originally intended by tonnage has been, and still is, the only term by which we form an idea of the magnitude, or, rather the dimensions of vessels. A law to be established for tonnage admeasurement would have reference only to cargo, and that in its simplest consideration, namely, the greatest weight which a vessel could safely carry."

Moorsom says that the first official measurements of vessels were of those carrying coal, and the date 1422; that in 1694 a government official marked the draft with nails on the stem and stern, by first loading to those marks by a dead weight of tin or lead. In 1720 the English Parliament, under the influence of competition of the tonnage dues being evaded by small vessels bringing spirits into the kingdom, passed this general law for tonnage: "The length of the keel (so much as she trends on the ground) is to be multiplied by the inside midship breadth and the whole divided by 94: the quotient is to be considered the true contents of the tonnage." By acts of 1773 the extreme or external breadth was substituted for the internal breadth; the length of the keel to be three-fifths of the extreme breadth, deducted from the length from the front of the stem to the aft side of the stern post. This law remained in force until the admeasurement of the cubic contents was substituted, by England in 1835–1855, and the United States in 1864.

In the fifth volume of Pepys's *Miscellany*, p. 57, date 1652, the dimensions of the Greyhound are given: Length of keel, 60 feet; breadth, 20 feet 3 inches; depth, 10 feet; burthen, 120 tons; men, 80; guns, 18. This vessel was in the old war which began in 1652, and in Pepys's Memoirs relating to the state of the navy in 1688, this vessel was then at sea.

If we apply the act of Parliament of 1720 to the dimensions of this vessel, subtracting 1.65 feet from breadth as an allowance for thickness of sides, to obtain inside breadth, the result is 120 tons, which shows that the act of 1720 only *confirmed* the *usage* of 1652.

Applying this act to Jal's vessel of 27^m 77^c length, and 8^m 12^c breadth, we have a vessel 91 feet long, 75 feet keel, 26$\frac{7}{10}$ beam, and 13 feet hold, measuring 254 tons, manifestly too large for Columbus's flag ship.

Spain exported wine in the fifteenth century, as now, and the old English expression of a tun of wine meant two pipes, 252 gallons, each gallon=231 cubic inches. Taking a gallon of wine at 8.33 pounds, this makes a ton only 2,099 pounds, but the difference to reach 2,240 was probably an allowance for the interstices of the casks.

If the ship used by Columbus on his first voyage was called either by him or his contemporaries, in round numbers, 100 tons, it was probably the expression of the dimensions of vessels which traded to England with wine and paid tonnage dues there, which was a specific sum for every tun of wine imported into the kingdom. Therefore, if the act of 1720, and Pepys's dimensions of the Greyhound,

---

[1] Cubit is generally stated to be 18 English inches; old Paris foot=12.789.—F. A. P. Barnard, in *Johnson's Universal Cyclopædia*.

1652, which agree, are used to find the dimensions of the hundred-ton vessel ascribed to Columbus, we get: length on deck, 63 feet; length of keel, 51 feet; extreme breadth, 20 feet; inside breadth for tonnage, 18 feet 6 inches; depth of hold, 10 feet, and draft of water, 10 feet 6 inches. These make a vessel of 100$\frac{34}{94}$ tons.

The rig of the Santa Maria is mentioned in the journal of October 24 (*Navarrete*, p. 39, and ~28 *ante*, p. ~~334~~) and this is all the information I can find bearing upon the subject. Columbus wrote: "I carried all the sails of the ship, the main sail, ~~and~~ two bonnets, the fore sail, and sprit-sail, and the mizen, and the main top sail." This omission of a foretop sail seems strange to our nautical ideas, but vessels similarly rigged are to be seen on the Ortelius' map, *Theatrum Orbis Terrarum*, Antwerp, 1570. Sprit-sails have been dispensed with in modern times, only since the steeve of bowsprits has been lessened and the size of jibs increased.

I finished a cruise around the world in the United States brigantine Dolphin, which had a length from front of the stem, under bowsprit, to inside of stern post of 88 feet; breadth of beam outside, 25 feet; inside, 23; depth of hold, 10 feet; draft aft, 10 feet; forward 8 feet, including the keel, which was 1 foot 6 inches. By Pepy's dimensions and the act of 1720, the Dolphin would be 205 tons. Her armament was two 9-pounders and eight 24-pound carronades. Officers and crew, 70. Foretop masthead 71 feet 6 inches above the water, and maintop masthead 81 feet 6 inches. I assume for the masthead lookout of the admiral's ship a height of 60 feet above the sea.

His vessel probably carried four anchors and they all used hemp cables. February 20, at the Azores, returning from his first voyage, he mentions that the cables were chafed off by the rocks and he put to sea. Fourth voyage—*Major*, p. 194: "I anchored at an island where I lost at one stroke three anchors. * * * The *single*(¹) anchor that remained to me."

They had pumps—*Major*, p. 195: "With three pumps, and the use of pots and kettles, we could scarcely, with all hands, clear the water that came into the ship."

Rudders.—The ancient way to steer was with two large paddles, one thrust through a port ~but~ ~bc~ on each quarter. The hinged rudder had come into use in Columbus's time. (See figure of a ship with both, in *Peregrinatio ad Terram Sanctam*, of Breydenbach, Mentz, 1486.)

Boats.—From a careful study of the narrative and words of Columbus I infer that his vessel and also the caravels each had but one boat. October 14 (*ante*, p. 14): "At dawn I ordered the boat of the ship." When his vessel was wrecked, on Christmas eve, 1492, the journal of December 25 says that the boat was got out to lay an anchor astern, but deserted to the Niña, whose commander sent it back with his own to render assistance. It appears from the journal of January 2 that the Admiral left to the colony of Navidad, among other things from the Santa Maria, "the boat of the ship." In the narrative of Diego Mendez—*Major*, p. 220—Mendez wrote with respect to the capture of the boats of the caravels in a river in Veragua, that the three vessels of the Admiral were at sea without boats, which would have been unlikely if any one had carried a spare boat. On his fourth voyage—*Major*, p. 177: "The ship which we had the greatest fear for had put out to sea for safety and reached the island of Gallega, having lost her boat and a greater part of her provisions." When he was at the Azores, February 19, on his return voyage, the Portuguese governor seized the boat and half the crew of the Niña, who were on shore at their devotions, and the Admiral got under way *in his vessel* to open a view of the town, to see what had become of it.

There is a decided difference of opinion in enumerating the number of persons with Columbus on his first voyage. Ferdinand Columbus wrote that 90 went in the three vessels; Peter Martyr and Giustiniani, 120; Jal, p. 228, that he left at Bohio 55 men, and returned to Spain with about 125, making 180 in all; Las Casas, *Navarrete*, vol. i, pp. 121–122, that he left in the island of Española, which the Indians called Bohio, thirty-nine men; Diego de Arana, Pedro Gutierrez, Rodrigo Escovedo, "with all the powers he held from their Highnesses." A notary and constable, carpenter and caulker, gunner and machinist, cooper, physician, and tailor, "and all, he said, that men of the sea."

This enumeration makes 48; but the true one is probably given in *Navarrete*, vol. 2, p. 19, note: 40 men and the 3 lieutenants, or 43 in all. In the journal of December 26, 1492, we notice that after the shipwreck many of the crew asked the Admiral for permission to remain until his return

---

(¹) *Italics* by the writer.

from Spain, and on the 2d of January it is recorded that he left with them all the goods sent for trafficking, and everything belonging to the wreckéd vessel, besides biscuit and wine for a year, and provisions. We learn from *Major*, p. 82, that his stores comprised biscuit, corn, wine, pork, and salt beef. Bernaldez says he took ten Indians with him to Spain. Martin Alonso Pinzon had deserted with the Pinta before the shipwreck, and, since Columbus believed him to be on his way to Spain, he acted as though he had only the little Niña with which to finish the voyage. In these circumstances it is a reasonable belief that, on account of space, if for no other reason, he must have left at Navidad at least as many persons as composed the crew of the wrecked vessel.

February 19, at the Azores, he sent half of the crew of the Niña on shore to perform a vow in a church; one boat from this vessel, which was the smallest of his squadron, took all. This implies that the crew were few. These facts persuade me to adopt the enumeration of Ferdinand Columbus, 90 persons for the three vessels. The inscription in the pavement of the cathedral of Seville is: *Con tres galeras y 90 personas.*

Neither Spain nor America has founded any enduring memorial to Christopher Columbus.

www.ingramcontent.com/pod-product-compliance
Lightning Source LLC
Chambersburg PA
CBHW022017080426

42733CB00007B/631